T0078106

Also read Fr. Mackin's
A Spirituality for Sunday People (Year B)

INTEGRITY:
LIVING GOD'S
WORD

Year C

FR. KEVIN E. MACKIN, OFM

WESTBOW
PRESS®
A DIVISION OF THOMAS NELSON
& ZONDERVAN

Scripture texts in this work are taken from the New American Bible, revised edition© 2010, 1991, 1986, 1970 Confraternity of Christian Doctrine, Washington, D.C. and are used by permission of the copyright owner. All Rights Reserved. No part of the New American Bible may be reproduced in any form without permission in writing from the copyright owner.

The writings of Mother Teresa of Calcutta © by the Mother Teresa Center, exclusive licensee throughout the world of the Missionaries of Charity for the works of Mother Teresa. Used with permission.

WestBow Press books may be ordered through booksellers or by contacting:

WestBow Press
A Division of Thomas Nelson & Zondervan
1663 Liberty Drive
Bloomington, IN 47403
www.westbowpress.com
1 (866) 928-1240

ISBN: 978-1-9736-1122-6 (sc)
ISBN: 978-1-9736-1124-0 (hc)
ISBN: 978-1-9736-1123-3 (e)

Library of Congress Control Number: 2017919637

Print information available on the last page.

WestBow Press rev. date: 01/02/2018

Dedicated to four Franciscan friars (among many)
who have made a difference in my life and ministry:

Damian Blaher brought common sense to my
pastoral questions.

Finian Kerwin let the fresh breezes of Vatican II
into the stodgy structures of my Franciscan life.

Vincent Cushing championed the Council's vision
of the church and world in that life.

Anthony Carrozzo emphasized the inseparability
of fraternity and ministry.

CONTENTS

INTRODUCTION

M any times, I have heard comments such as, "I really like my church community; we are welcoming, there's lively participation, good preaching, and I'm encountering the living Christ in the word and in the breaking of the bread. I leave eager to do good for others."

I like to hear these comments from active participants striving to live God's word with integrity. Who are we, this global network of parishes? We believe that the celebration of the Mass or the Eucharist is "the source and summit of the Christian life" (*Lumen Gentium*). It's the source from which we draw our spiritual nourishment, and it's the summit, the high point in our community of disciples. We truly encounter the living Christ in the Eucharist: body and blood, soul and divinity. The appearances remain, but the essence becomes the real presence of the living Christ.

We believe in God as Triune and in Jesus Christ as Son of God and redeemer of humankind. Celebrating this belief ritually in the Mass, we recognize the bishop of Rome in his Petrine ministry as the foundation of "the unity of bishops and laity." This community views reality primarily in a threefold manner: it sees God in all things (sacramentality); it encounters God through fellow human beings and material elements (mediation); and it embraces the unity of God's creation (communion).

Most of us are familiar with the liturgical year and with the order of the Mass: the introductory rites (penitential rite, opening prayer); the Liturgy of the Word; and the Liturgy of the Eucharist (preparing gifts, the Eucharistic Prayer, the Communion rite, and the concluding rite).

Eucharist—a word from the Greek expression for being grateful—is at the center of our lives. When Jesus called the disciples together for a

Last Supper, it is clear he wanted the occasion / the purpose to coincide with Passover. It is important to situate it as Jesus did. The purpose of the Passover was to reexperience the meal the Hebrews ate centuries before in Egypt. At the time of the Exodus, it was a hasty meal; at the time of Jesus, a solemn and grateful meal, thanking God for our gifts.

The first course of Passover, bitter herbs dipped in vinegar sauce, was a reminder of the bitterness of their slavery. Then the main course was the lamb whose blood marked their doors as the angel of death passed over their homes in Egypt. Beginning with the main course, the head of the family blessed the bread, broke it, and shared it with each at the table. He then blessed the cup and shared it.

We can easily fit the Gospel narrative in the Passover setting: Judas left after the first course; Christ washed the feet of the disciples before the main course; and the words over bread and wine are clearly from the blessing that began and ended the main course. The word Passover came from the Hebrew word *pesach*. The Greek translation was *pascha*, and the meal came to be called the Paschal meal.

The Eucharist communicates two realities. First, Jesus gives his life for his disciples. The separation of the bread and wine expresses separation of the body from the blood: in other words, death. Jesus gives his body and blood, his life, as a sacrifice of reconciliation, not to appease an angry God but as proof of God's love for us, to show that this God of love desires the reconciliation of all human beings. God sent his only Son to be the servant who sacrifices himself in place of his brothers/ sisters. Jesus's blood seals the new covenant.

The Eucharist also communicates a second reality. Jesus gives his life as food. We are in the midst of a meal. By eating the bitter herbs, the unleavened bread, and the lamb, the Hebrews associated themselves with the Exodus. The words said over the different foods gave the foods a new power, so much so that by eating, the guests benefited anew from the favors their forebears received. Jesus commands his disciples to renew his action. It is not simply a commemoration of a departed friend but the renewal of a sacred action by which God's sacrifice is made present through the bread and wine.

Jesus instituted the Eucharist because he wished to remain with us until the end-time, not only through the presence of his spirit but also through his body, crucified and risen. The Eucharist brings the presence of the living Christ here and now, between the past of the Crucifixion/Resurrection and the future of our heavenly glory, a real presence whereby we experience the living Christ. And since the living Christ is the nucleus of the new order, this mystery brings a collective presence whereby we meet in the living Christ the whole of his body, the church.

The Christ we meet in the Eucharist is the Christ who died and rose from the dead and who will raise us up—the real presence of Christ. Bread and wine mystically become Christ, body and blood, soul and divinity. When the living Christ communicates his life to us, it is our bodies as much as our souls that *He unites with himself in order to recreate us.*

The living Christ is really present. Unless you eat his flesh and drink his blood, you will not have life in you. Yes, it is the living Christ, transformed from mortality to immortality, corruption to incorruptibility, mystically present to us. How can this be? It is a mystery of faith. We believe because we believe in the all-powerful and ever-creative Word of God.

When we receive the living Christ, we do not receive him alone. For Christ carries in himself the whole of humanity, of which he is the head. We are reconciled with God and one another. The humanity of Christ, body and soul, is a melting pot in which God is recasting his work. This work applies to all human beings, in every age. The living Christ must touch each person who comes into the world. Christ makes us members of his body through this contact, bearing within himself all humanity. Since the sacraments give us the living Christ, they unite us by that fact to all humanity. In the Eucharist, we meet one another united by the love of Christ. That is why the Eucharist is the sacrament of love.

What is the purpose? To form us into one faith community. Paul wrote: "Because the loaf of bread is one, we, though many, are one body, for we all partake of the one loaf" (1 Cor 10:17). And this bread we eat and this blood we drink should not only form us into a community of deeper faith but also should empower us to reach out compassionately to the people around us. Yes, the Eucharist is a going forth. We must go from the church to wash the feet of our brothers and sisters in daily life.

In giving ourselves to others, we will be freed. We will experience the Exodus anew. We will live God's word and act with integrity wherever we are, and whatever our profession and relationships.

Reflecting on the word of God within the three-year liturgical cycle, this collection of homilies hopes to touch the hearts and minds of disciples of Jesus who have already heard the universal call to holiness.

I am grateful for Janet Gianopoulos, whose assistance and attention to detail contributed to the tasks of preparing this book.

First Sunday of Advent

Today's Gospel reminds me of the fellow who lived recklessly all his life: ate and drank and partied day in and day out. Eventually, he was dying. The family called the pastor of the parish, who began to celebrate the rite of reconciliation. And in the course of the rite, the pastor asked, "Do you renounce Satan?" There was silence. A second time, the pastor asked in a louder voice, "Do you renounce Satan?" Still, there was silence. Finally, the pastor shouted, "Do you renounce Satan?" And the fellow slowly opened his eyes and said, "Look, in my condition, I don't want to antagonize anyone at this time." Now that's hedging one's bet.

Let me begin with a true story. A man read that, according to the local newspaper, he had died. Actually, his older brother had died, but the editors ran the wrong article. The man was fascinated to find out what people thought of him. But what he read shocked him. The obituary reported the passing of a "great industrialist" who amassed a considerable fortune from manufacturing weapons of unimaginable destruction in those days—dynamite. His reputation as a heartless employer and ruthless businessman was also chronicled. The newspaper ended its story calling him a "merchant of death."

The man was stunned. This was not how he wanted to be remembered. From that moment on, he devoted his time and fortune to works of philanthropy, justice, and peace.

Today, he is not remembered as the inventor of weapons but as the founder of the prestigious Nobel Prizes. Alfred Nobel would later say, "Everyone ought to have the chance to correct his or her epitaph in midstream and write a new one." And when Nobel actually died in 1896, his obituary hailed him as "a humanitarian and a visionary."

We might want to ask ourselves in light of the word of God, how do we want to be remembered? As someone who made a difference for the better in people's lives? The choice is ours.

Advent invites us to reflect on the threefold coming of Jesus. Jesus came to us centuries ago in Bethlehem of Judea as the Word made flesh; He comes to us now sacramentally and mystically in the signs of bread and wine; and he will come again triumphantly at the end of time. And so how might we celebrate Advent? Some families create an advent wreath and light one candle at the dinner table during the first week, two candles during the second week, and so on. And after lighting the candle, they pray in their own words for the coming anew of the Messiah into their own lives. Other families make a Jesse or genealogy tree to reexperience the story of our salvation, and still other families set up a Nativity scene and invite family members to take turns telling in their own words the meaning of Christmas or God-with-us, Emmanuel. These are but a few family customs that can help us keep alive the meaning of Advent this year.

Now the word of God carries us back in our imaginations to a prophet named Jeremiah. The sixth century, the 500s, was a catastrophe for the Hebrews. Ancient Babylonia leveled the city of Jerusalem, tore down the temple, and deported many Hebrews to Babylonia. For this calamity, Jeremiah cited the infidelity of the Hebrews to their covenantal promises. But God, Jeremiah proclaimed, is always faithful. And so Jeremiah spoke about hope: God one day will raise up a new king who will do what is right and good for his people (Jer 33:14–16). And as we reflect upon this, we might ask ourselves, do we try our best to do the right thing?

Paul in his letter to the Christian community at Thessalonika in Greece urged them not to so much anticipate the "world to come" that they forget how to live here and now. Yes, Paul wrote, care for one another, pray fervently, please God, and be ready when the Day of the Lord comes to us in the mystery of death. Paul might say to you and me today, Jesus comes to us every day in the many opportunities we have to do good for one another (1 Thes 3:12–4:2).

In the Gospel according to Luke, Jesus spoke dramatically about signs (skies darkening, waters raging, winds roaring), signs that will signal the coming of Christ with great power and glory (Lk 21:25–28, 34–36). And so, Jesus said, "Change your ways; turn toward a God-centered life, an other-centered life." Surely we do not want Christ to chide us: "I was hungry, and you bought a Ferrari. I was thirsty, and you hoisted your tenth Bud. I was lonely in a hospital or nursing home, and you were too overcommitted to see me."

We gather together in his name around the table of the Lord to hear God's voice in scripture and to reexperience the sacrificial, life-giving death and glorious resurrection of Jesus. And through this mystery, we have become by grace what Jesus Christ is by nature: sons and daughters of God. And that great truth of our faith (God within us, sons and daughters of God) challenges us especially this Advent season to always look for the good not only in ourselves but in other people and in the everyday situations of life.

Be a good-finder this Advent season. Someone who looks for the good in oneself, in other people, and in the situations of life. Remember that magnificent hymn of the Virgin Mary:

> My Soul proclaims the greatness of the Lord;
> my spirit rejoices in God my savior.
> Because He the Mighty One has done great things for me.

The beautiful canticle of Mary appears in Luke, chapter 1, verses 46–55. Mary rejoiced in the gifts God gave her, and so too should we rejoice in the gifts God has given us and use them for others.

Look for the good in other people. Someone wrote that people in many ways are like wildflowers. We can easily them for granted. But if you ever picked a wildflower and studied it, you would discover the veins, the fragile petals, the beautiful blossom. If you turn it toward the sunlight, you will discover its special symmetry. The wildflower has a beauty all its own. And so too do people.

Finally, look for good in the myriad situations of life. When one door closes, another door usually opens if we pay attention. Remember, God is the ultimate good-finder. God so loved us that he became one of us. Think of all the people of the Gospel that he met; he found goodness in all of them.

Pray this Advent season that God will help those who doubt to find faith; those who despair to find hope; those who are weak to find courage; those who are sick to find healing; those who are sad or depressed or angry to find joy; those who wander to find the way; and those who have died to find eternal life in God.

Second Sunday of Advent

I read about an Air Lingus flight from Ireland to Greece. Thirty minutes out, a flight attendant made the following announcement in her Irish brogue: "Ladies and gentlemen, I'm so sorry, but there has been a terrible mix-up. We have a hundred passengers, and unfortunately, we received only fifty meals. I truly apologize." When passengers' muttering died down, she continued, "Anyone kind enough to give up a meal will receive free unlimited drinks for the duration of our four-hour flight." Her next announcement came two hours later. "We still have those fifty dinners available." I guess the moral of the story is be careful what you offer!

The word of God takes us back to Baruch, in the sixth century before Jesus. That century, we know, was a catastrophe for ancient Israel; everything the Jews thought would endure forever suddenly disappeared. Yet, in the midst of this catastrophe, Baruch spoke about hope: a splendid new Jerusalem, a faithful people who will reflect the glory of God in their daily lives and who will be instruments of forgiveness, compassion, generosity, honesty, joy, peace, and love. The word of God may be asking us whether we are such instruments (Bar 5:1–9).

Paul, in his letter to the Christian community at Philippi in Greece, prayed that we will possess true wisdom, the wisdom to distinguish what matters from what doesn't matter, so that we will always choose right over wrong. What do we value most? Paul asks. Our relationship with God and one another. Paul may be asking whether we pray for the wisdom to know what truly matters in life (Phil 1:4–6, 8–11).

And in the Gospel according to Luke, John the Baptizer appeared, proclaiming repentance: prepare our hearts for the Lord. In other words, help us to hear the word of God in our hearts and turn away from a self-centered life to a God-centered life, an other-centered life, so that we may see clearly the way to walk, the truth to speak, and the life to live. The word of God may be asking whether we, like John the Baptizer, are preparing ourselves afresh to let Jesus, the Christ, into our lives (Lk 3:1–6).

The Hebrews throughout the centuries prayed for the Messiah to come to them. This is what Advent is all about—praying for the Messiah to come. Yes, the Hebrews waited: in the Exodus from ancient Egypt; in the rise and fall of their kings; in their exile in Babylonia; and in their sufferings throughout foreign occupations. And yet the Messiah did not come to rescue them, especially in their tragedies.

In many ways, we are like those Hebrews; we often pray for God to come to us, to rescue us from a crisis of one kind or another—for example, a life-threatening illness, or a shattered family relationship, or a workplace crisis, or a family addiction. Many may have asked the question in the massacres of innocent people, where was God? I think of the Christians who lost innocent loved ones in the mindless violence of ISIS in Syria or in Iraq or Libya. Perhaps those innocent Christians in the moment of their dying even asked God to rescue them. And yet God seemed to be hidden from them.

We, too, beg God to rescue us. In fact, this is the story of everyone. For sometimes we seem to walk in darkness; yes, we seem to experience not the presence but the absence of God. And even if we don't experience the absence, we are forever searching for God, but God is forever looking for us.

Sometimes God does seem silent. But is God hidden? Is he silent? Our faith proclaims loudly that God is indeed in our midst. Not in a manger. That happened centuries ago in Bethlehem. God is all around us—in people and in nature, in a sunrise and sunset, in landscapes and waterscapes, in the snow of winter and the heat of summer.

He is in our midst right now. In this community of faith, wherever two or three are gathered in his name, there God is. He is in the word proclaimed; he is sacramentally and mystically in the bread and wine.

He is deep within ourselves, at the core of own being. We cannot touch God. And yet he is here, in all of us gathered together as a faith community.

And what does all of this mean—God-with-us, Emmanuel? St. Paul wrote: God's favor has been revealed to us in Jesus. God so loves us that he gave his only Son in the mystery of the incarnation. Jesus, crucified and risen, anticipates what we will become. And until he comes, you and I are to continue his ministry on earth, to reach out to people with the helping hand of forgiveness, compassion, generosity, honesty, joy, peace, and love.

Let me close with an observation about gifts. Many of us have begun our holiday shopping and may be spending more time than we should in search of that perfect gift for someone else. Often, we're not sure whether that gift is what that someone else needs or even wants.

Marian Wright Edelman, a well-known children's advocate and author, recalls that the best presents she received as a child were not toys wrapped in pretty boxes. From her father, she received a love of reading. For him, books to improve the mind were more important than toys. And from her mother, young Marian received a passion for children's rights. Her mother asked her—and she wasn't very happy about it—to share her room with a homeless child, and this was one of nearly a dozen foster brothers and sisters her mother raised. And from a neighbor, Marian received the gift of courage not to be afraid when something important or good had to be done.

Edelman writes in her autobiography, *From Lanterns: A Memoir of Mentors*, "Like many of us, I no longer remember most of the presents I found under the tree as a child. But I carry with me and treasure the lessons in life my parents and my caring neighbors gave me throughout my childhood. And may these memories give me the strength to give a child a true gift—time spent with a child, time spent reading with children some of the great lives of mentors who have enriched, informed and helped shape my life."

Yes, some gifts really can transform the lives of the people we love: gifts of teaching, of listening and supporting, gifts of sharing our time and our experiences, gifts of compassion and forgiveness and affirmation. And this begins in our own families and our workplaces.

So, this holiday season, I hope all of us will think of those enduring gifts that we can always give to one another, gifts that cost little to nothing, gifts that can transform the lives of the people whom we love, especially our families.

And especially this season, we pray, come, Lord Jesus. Transform us into new creatures and renew this planet of ours.

THIRD SUNDAY OF ADVENT

This Sunday is known as Gaudete Sunday. Gaudete is a Latin verb that means "rejoice." We rejoice because our salvation is near. The Messiah is about to come.

The point is that we have so much to be thankful for, including family, faith, and friends. A colleague e-mailed a poem about joy that he read in a book by Og Mandino, author of *The Greatest Salesman in the World*. So many people lack what we take for granted. Here are a few lines:

> With feet to take me where I'd go ...
> with eyes to see the sunset's glow ...
> With ears to hear what I need to know.
> Oh, God, forgive me when I whine.
> I've been blessed indeed. The world is mine.

This season is indeed a time to count our blessings.

The word of God takes us back to the seventh century before Jesus: the 600s. The author of the book of Zephaniah sang a hymn of freedom from tyranny. Shout for joy, sing joyfully, be glad, the author proclaimed. Why? Because God was near to the faithful Hebrews, and they will rebuild their city of Jerusalem and its temple (Zep 3:14–18). The word of God may be asking us whether we realize that God also is near to us, especially in rough and tough times.

Paul, in his letter to the Christian community at Philippi in Greece, urged them to be joyful and generous in their relationships with one another, to pray confidently to God, and not to be anxious about their lives (Phil 4:4–7).

By the way, a friend advised me, "Don't worry. Remember, Moses started as a basket case."

Yes, the word of God invites us to cast our worries upon God because he cares for us.

And in the Gospel according to Luke, John the Baptizer preached repentance. Share with the needy; be fair and honest in business dealings; don't be greedy. John went on to say, "One mightier than I is coming. I am not worthy to loosen the thongs of his sandals. He will baptize you with the holy Spirit and fire" (Lk 3:10–18).

During this Advent season, the word of God focuses primarily on three biblical personalities: Isaiah, John the Baptizer, and the Virgin Mary. There's an ancient wisdom tradition that says God sends each person into this life with a special message to deliver, with a special song to sing for others, with a special act of love to bestow. All three biblical personalities, in their awesome experience of God, delivered a special message, sang a special song, and bestowed a special act of love.

The author of Isaiah described a Messiah who would be a liberator, a redeemer, a savior. John the Baptizer, at the waters of the Jordan River, pointed to Jesus as the Lamb of God. The lamb of course references the Hebrew Passover meal, the Seder service. Jesus is the sacrificial Lamb who through his own death and resurrection reestablished our relationship with God.

The Virgin Mary is the living temple of God, the ark of the Hebrew covenant, because she carried within herself the unique presence of God, the Word made flesh, a child, Emmanuel, God-with-us, the God-man, Jesus of Nazareth.

I would like to tell you a true story about a schoolteacher named Jean Thompson and a fifth-grade student called Teddy. Miss Thompson had a special message to deliver, a special song to sing, and a special act of love to bestow upon Teddy.

On the first day of school, she told her students, "I love you all the same," but she knew it didn't quite ring true. Little Teddy didn't seem to pay attention, wore messy and dirty clothes, and, unknown to her, had a learning disability. As the semester progressed, Jean Thompson's reports about Teddy were not positive: "not a good home situation; mother terminally ill; mother dies; father doesn't seem to care, needs help," and so on.

When the Christmas holidays came, the fifth graders brought little gifts to Jean's desk, all wrapped in brightly colored paper, except for Teddy's. His was wrapped in brown paper held together with Scotch tape. Scribbled in crayon were the words, "For Miss Thompson from Teddy." She opened the brown paper, and out fell a bracelet with most of the stones missing, and an almost empty bottle of ordinary perfume. When the youngsters began to giggle, Jean put some of the perfume on her wrist, put on the bracelet, held her wrist up to the children, and said, "Doesn't it smell lovely? Isn't the bracelet pretty?" Taking their cue from their teacher, they all agreed.

At the end of the day, when the children left, Teddy lingered, came over to her desk, and said, "Miss Thompson, all day long you smelled just like my mother. And her bracelet, that's her bracelet, it looks nice on you, and I'm really happy you like my presents." When Teddy left, she buried her head on her desk and cried.

The next day, when the children arrived, Jean's attitude toward Teddy changed. She always cared for all of her students, but now she helped Teddy catch up to the other students.

Time passed, and Jean lost track of Teddy. Seven years later, she received this note: "Dear Miss Thompson: I'm graduating from high school, and I'm second in my class. I wanted you to be the first to know. Love, Teddy." Four years later, there was another note: "Dear Miss Thompson: I wanted you to be the first to know. College has not been easy, but I'm graduating. Love, Teddy Stollard." And four years later: "Dear Miss Thompson: As of today, I am Dr. Theodore J. Stollard. How about that? I wanted you to be the first to know. I'm going to be married in July. And I want you to come and sit where my mother would have sat, because you're the only family I have. Dad died last year."

And Jean Thompson went, and she sat where his mother would have sat. She was a decent and loving human being who reached out to a student when he needed help, and she set him on a career path where he could do much good for others.

You and I know that there are millions of children all over this nation, children who are left out and left back, who will never become doctors or lawyers or teachers or professionals or much else, partly because there was no person with a heart to make a difference. This was a story at the elementary-school level, but at all levels we need to be reminded that the very same miracles happen and that we can help to make them happen.

Like Isaiah, John, the Virgin Mary, and that schoolteacher, God has called us to deliver a special message, sing a special song, and bestow a special act of love upon others. What is that message, song, and act of love?

FOURTH SUNDAY OF ADVENT

A few years ago, I attended a Christmas luncheon of alumni from my alma mater. These alums were bragging about their children. "My daughter is a professor," one alum said. "When she enters a room, everyone says, 'Hello, Professor.'" Another alum said, "My son is an academic vice president at a college. When he enters a room, everyone says, 'Hello, Mr. Vice President.'" Still another thought hard and then said, "My son is four feet eight inches tall and weighs six hundred pounds. When he enters a room, everyone says, 'Oh, my God.'" So much for bragging rights.

The Christmas season is upon us. It's a time for family, a time for worship, and a time for friendship and celebration. Above all, it's a time for gratitude—gratitude to God for his many blessings.

The word of God takes us back to the eighth century before Jesus, to a prophet by the name of Micah. My favorite quote from Micah is: "Do what is right and love goodness, and walk humbly with your God." Today, Micah proclaimed that God's promise of a Messiah will be born in Bethlehem (where King David was born), and this Messiah will guide people securely and "he shall be peace" (Mi 5:1–4). This invites us to remember that God always keeps his promises, and so too should we. Try always to do the right thing.

The letter to the Hebrews compared the Jerusalem Temple sacrifices to the bodily death of Jesus on the cross. The author indicated Jesus's sacrificial death is far superior. Yes, Jesus, through his fidelity to his heavenly Father and through his own self-giving, opened up to us eternal life. The

13

word invites us to be faithful to our baptismal promises and to live a God-centered, other-centered life in service to one another (Heb 10:5–10).

Some of you may recognize the name of Albert Schweitzer. He was a theologian and musician and made extraordinary contributions in both disciplines. But then he decided to become a medical doctor, to serve in remote West Africa. With a medical degree in hand, Schweitzer established a hospital in Lambarene, Gabon, in 1913. He was later awarded the Nobel Peace Prize for his humanitarian work. Asked for his motto, Schweitzer's answer to students was, "Service. Let this word accompany each of you throughout your life. Let it be before you as you seek your way and your duty in the world. May it be recalled to your minds if ever you are tempted to forget it or set it aside. It will not always be a comfortable companion but it will always be a faithful one. And it will lead you to happiness, no matter what the experiences of your lives." Albert Schweitzer indeed lived a God-centered, other-centered life; his philosophy of "reverence for life" extended to fellow human beings and to all animals.

In the Gospel according to Luke, we have the story of Mary's visit to her cousin Elizabeth. Both were pregnant—Mary with Jesus, Elizabeth with John the Baptizer. Elizabeth cried out, "Blessed are you among women, and blessed is the fruit of your womb" (Luke 1:42), and these words became part of our Hail Mary. Elizabeth recognized the presence of God in Mary, the living Ark of the Covenant (Lk 1:39–45).

The word challenges us to be generous with our time and talent and to recognize and revere the presence of God in all God's creation.

As we approach Christmas, I've been thinking of the December 2015 Paris Climate Agreement as well as Pope Francis's encyclical *Laudato Si* or *Praise Be to You, My Lord*. And then I remembered a classic film about the care of our common home, the earth, and our fellow inhabitants. The title of the film is *A Civil Action*. Some of you may have seen it. It's about a factory dumping toxic chemicals into the waters of Woburn, Massachusetts. The film is based on a true story that Jonathan Harr tells in a best seller by the same name.

In the film, John Travolta played Jan Schlichtmann, a Boston personal injury attorney. He's what you might call an ambulance chaser. He likes notoriety, two-thousand-dollar suits, five-hundred-dollar

14

shoes, silk ties, and gold watches. He defends victims against giant corporations—greedy ones, he says—and makes a huge profit.

But then came the Woburn case. The lawyer met with parents of children who had died of leukemia. The cause was toxic chemicals from a factory seeping into the town's well water. At first the lawyer told the parents the case wasn't worth fighting. But on the way home, he saw some bubbly water in the river. Intrigued, he muddied his expensive shoes, tracking the water to its source. And when he finally reached the tannery that had been dumping the toxic chemicals, his face lit up—not from solving the mystery but from discovering that the factory was linked to deep-pocket corporations. At first, he was in it for the money. He bet every cent he had on taking the case to the limit. For nine years, the case dragged on. The opposing attorneys wore him down through delays, legal hairsplitting, intimidating witnesses. And his own arrogance also got in the way. But what kept him going? When the going got tough, he drove back to the very spot on the highway where one of the children died in his parents' car before they could get him to the hospital. Without realizing it, the case now was not about money but about people; he wanted justice.

In the end, the Travolta character lost his firm, his home, and his expensive clothes and was forced to accept a settlement. But in the process of losing so much, he gradually was transformed from an ambulance chaser into a new man, a person of integrity and justice and compassion.

You may not be able to give your money, but you certainly can give your time and talent to help others. I truly believe that service—generosity with our time and talent—refreshes the soul.

And until Jesus comes again in great glory and power, we are called to continue the saving work of Jesus Christ. May this prayer be ours:

Lord, help all our loved ones to find peace;
Those who doubt to find faith …;
Those who despair to find hope …
Those who are weak to find courage …
Those who are sick to find health …

Those who are sad and depressed to find joy ...
Those who wander to find the way ...
Those who are angry to find a way to let go ...
Those who have died to find their rest in the embrace of God.

The Nativity of the Lord

M erry Christmas, feliz Navidad, joyeux Noel, buon Natale, frohe Weihnacten! A blessed and happy Christmas to each and every one.

One day, a wealthy man took his son on a trip to show how poor people live. They spent a couple of days and nights on a farm. On their return home, the father asked his son, "How was the trip?" "Great, Dad." "Did you see how poor people live?" the father asked. "Yes," said the son. "So, tell me, what did you learn?" asked the father. The son answered, "I saw that we have one dog, and they have four. We have a pool in the middle of our garden, and they have a creek that has no end. We have imported lanterns, and they have the stars at night. Our patio reaches to the front yard, and they have the whole horizon. We have a small piece of land to live on, and they have fields that go on beyond our sight. We have servants who serve us; they serve others. We buy our food; they grow theirs. We have walls to protect us; they have friends to protect them." The boy's father was speechless. Then his son added, "Thanks, Dad, for showing me how poor we are."

Isn't perspective a wonderful thing? It makes you wonder what would happen if we all gave thanks for everything we have. Christmas invites us to appreciate our life, our family, our faith, our home, our job, our friends, and on and on. Yes, give thanks to God for blessing us in so many different and wonderful ways.

When we really stop and think about it, we are indeed blessed. A popular Broadway song goes, "We need a little Christmas, right this very minute." Never truer than this year. A holiday of hope. At the heart of the Christmas season is the very word holiday: holy day. And what is holiness? It is a journey, a pilgrimage, a moving toward a relationship with God forever.

I think of a special journey to the small town of Bethlehem in what we call today the Middle East. In the humblest of surroundings, amidst a small family and fellow creatures, the Christ Child was born over two thousand years ago. The Word of God became flesh and made his dwelling among us.

Many centuries later, in 1223, St. Francis of Assisi set out for the town of Greccio to celebrate Christmas in a special way. Francis wanted to relive the experience of the Christ Child in a real manger, with real people, a real ox and donkey, and real shepherds. So he set up a nativity scene. Francis wanted everyone to share in the joy of Christmas. He wanted the poor and the hungry to sit down with the rich. He included animals, who figure so importantly in the first hours Jesus spent on earth, in a manger, a feeding trough for animals. The people then worked to bring forth St. Francis's vision of Christmas. Candles lit the night, lights appeared in the valley, and people began to walk toward Greccio so that they could "adore the Christ Child." And Francis, vested as a deacon, sang the beautiful lesson that told of a mother who "gave birth to her first-born child and wrapped him in swaddling clothes and laid him in a manger ..."

That night, wrote biographer Thomas of Celano, "Greccio was transformed into a second Bethlehem, and that wonderful night seemed like fullest day to both man and beast for the joy." And these people had such a deeply religious experience of Christmas at Greccio that the Franciscan friars began to popularize this Christmas night wherever they went, a great tradition that continues to this day.

This holiday season, I invite all of us to reawaken and nurture the life of God within us. All of us, all things and all creatures, belong to the family of an all-good and compassionate God. Christmas especially is a time to renew our faith, to be grateful for the precious life God has given us, and to enjoy the company of one another in our family gathering. It's a time to rededicate ourselves to creating a more joyful and peaceful family life. In the tradition of St. Francis, let us celebrate "God-with-us," Emmanuel. In our struggle to find purpose in life, God is with us; in the messes we make of our lives and the messes others make, so to speak, God is with us. Despite our forgetting and abandoning God, God neither forgets nor abandons us; and despite suffering, there is the hope of resurrection.

The meaning of Christmas can be summed up in a single line from the prologue of the Gospel according to John: "The Word became flesh and made his dwelling among us." That is the wonder of Christmas. God touched us in a newborn infant, in a feeding trough for animals, in a forgotten corner of God's good earth. Why? "God so loved the world" (Jn 3:6). This child brought new life to a dying world, and by dying and rising restored God's life in us. That's the message of Christmas.

There's a tradition that says the Christ Child was born in a stable. A stable is a haven for animals and a storehouse for harvests. Children find them special places of play. Stables are places where every dimension of life and death is played out: new calves are born, young chickens are nurtured, sick horses are cared for. Stables can also be untidy, even in these days of recycling and repurposing.

And yet, in the Christmas moment, God transformed a humble stable into the holiest of shrines. In many ways, our lives are like that, filled with all the joy and pain that challenge us to grow and fulfill our dreams. The Christ born in Bethlehem came to bring light and life and love to each one of us. And if God could be born in such a place, that same God can be born in us. And that's what Christmas is all about—God within each one of us. That great truth of our faith ought to challenge us always to be good-finders, looking for the good in ourselves, in other people, in the situations of life.

When the song of the angels is stilled, the shepherds are back with their flocks, the star in the sky is gone, and the wise men are home, only then does the work of Christmas begin. The work of Christmas entrusted to each of us is a daily invitation and a lifelong challenge to reveal Jesus to others and make his kingdom a reality. This calls us to heal wounds with kind words and helping hands; to ease pain with compassionate care; to renew hope with thoughtful encouragement; to restore happiness with our own inner joy; and to inspire trust in God with our own faith.

> May you be poor in misfortune this Christmas season
> And rich in blessing,
> Slow to make enemies,
> Quick to make friends,
> And rich or poor,
> Slow or quick,
> As happy as the new year is long!

The Holy Family of Jesus, Mary, and Joseph

I don't want to make the mistake Mark Twain heard a preacher make. Apparently, the preacher spoke eloquently about good works. Mark Twain was so moved that he decided to contribute ten dollars when the plate came around. But as the preacher kept on talking, Twain began to get a bit weary. After another five minutes, he decided ten dollars was too extravagant. By the time the preacher was finally through, Twain tossed a dime into the collection plate and dashed for the door.

So I'll be right to the point. Today we celebrate the Feast of the Holy Family of Jesus, Mary, and Joseph. And I begin with a true story.

Over a century and a half ago, diamond fever spread across the continent of Africa. Some people struck it rich. But for others, it became a long, disappointing search. One man wandered throughout Africa, finding nothing. Meanwhile, back on the land that man had sold, the new owner found a strange-looking stone in the small creek on the property. He placed it on his fireplace mantel as a curio. One day, a visitor noticed this stone. He shouted excitedly at the farmer, "Do you know this is a diamond? It's one of the largest I've ever seen." The entire farm was loaded with magnificent diamonds.

The point is this: some people never take the time to notice what they have in their own backyard, so to speak. Some people never notice the "gems" they have in their own families and in their parishes. So, stop and smell the roses in your own backyard. Notice the gem you have in your spouse and sons/daughters; and sons and daughters, notice the gem in your parents. And notice the gems in the parish. The word of God takes us back to the eleventh century before Jesus (the early 1000s), an unstable era in Hebrew history immediately before the establishment of their monarchy. A woman named Hannah prayed to God for a child. And God heard her prayer. She gave birth to Samuel, whom his parents offered for God's service in the shrine at Shiloh. Samuel, we know, grew up to become a great prophet who played a significant role in ancient Israel's affairs of state (1 Sm 1:20–22, 24–28).

The word of God invites us to make our needs known to God.

The author of the letter of John spoke about God's unconditional love for us. God has gifted us with divine status. We are his children, sons and daughters of God our Father, and our destiny is to be like God, to see God as God is. But here and now, our calling is to please God in our everyday attitudes and behaviors so that we can live in God and God in us. (1 Jn 3:1–2, 21–24).

And in the Gospel according to Luke, the family of Jesus, Mary, and Joseph went to the temple in Jerusalem. Jesus astonished the rabbis with his wisdom. On their way back from this pilgrimage, Mary and Joseph suddenly realized Jesus was missing. But their anxiety turned into joy when they found Jesus. This close-knit family went back home to Nazareth, where Jesus grew in wisdom and age and God's favor (Lk 2:41–52).

For twenty-some years, this family clung together. They fled to Egypt together. They lived in a backwater village and worked together at ordinary tasks. Joseph, tradition says, kept his loved ones in bread with the skill of his hands. Mary baked and spun, carried water, and taught Jesus to pray. They lived an utterly simple and natural and human life. And like every family, Mary eventually waved a goodbye to Jesus as he set off for his life's mission. She experienced the empty nest!

Theirs was a holy family, and so too is yours—living together, working together, playing and praying together. And what sustained this holy family in Nazareth? And what sustains ours? I would like to suggest three virtues: faithfulness, courage, and prudence.

Faithfulness: There's probably no virtue more important than faithfulness for sustaining family life. Married couples are called to be open to new life and to nourish and educate the children with whom God gifts them. To do this well, parents need to be faithful to each other and to their children. Faithfulness builds trust. Children, for example, trust that parents will always be there for them. We all need to know that someone loves us and will always be there for us, especially when we hit a rough patch in life. And yes, sometimes parents have to show tough love for the good of their children. But the point is we as families need the anchor of faithfulness in our ever-changing world.

Second, families need courage. In William Bennett's *Book of Virtues*, we find under the title "Courage" the stories of David and Goliath, Susan B. Anthony, and Rosa Parks. Courage is about moral character. It defines who we are at the core of our innermost selves. It is an attitude that challenges us, despite our fears, to stand up for what is right and true and good. Many of us would also include people such as Gandhi, Martin Luther King Jr, and Mother Teresa in our list of courageous people. And we probably would include our parents. We have seen up close the sacrifices our parents have made for us. Commitment to another, in good times and bad, requires courage. Parental courage reaches a crescendo when children become teenagers. Parents can't protect them from the many forces in society that can destroy teenagers not only physically but morally. Yes, children grow and age, and eventually parents must let them go. Parenting, sustaining life, more than any other activity, requires courage, always trying to do the right thing even when we're not sure it's the right thing. After all, to be human is to live in ambiguity.

And the third virtue is prudence. It doesn't mean caution. Rather it's an instinct to seek what's the right thing to do among our many choices, whereas courage is the instinct to do the right thing despite our fears. They go hand in hand. Parents have to act amid the messiness of everyday life. They are forced to make decisions often without clearly seeing all the possible outcomes. And often decisions are not either/or but both/and. That's why we sometimes must agree to disagree and move on with our lives. But it's only by making decisions daily that parents become experienced decision makers. Prudence requires that parents continually reflect on their decisions and learn from them for the future.

Someone wrote: "Twenty years from now, we will be more disappointed by the things we didn't do than by the ones we did." Think about it. Don't regret something you could have done but didn't; you only live once, as the saying goes. Everyday life is not a dress rehearsal; it's the real thing. To the extent that our lives are in our own hands, do good now, not later. Don't regret not doing it.

Jesus, Mary, and Joseph lived a life together as a family, a holy family, a life with no regrets. Faithfulness, courage, and prudence anchored that family. May God on this Feast of the Holy Family anchor our own families in faithfulness, courage, and prudence.

THE EPIPHANY OF THE LORD

I was with family in New York City, and somehow or other we ended up in a conversation about the origins of "little Christmas" and the Feast of the Epiphany. My sister commented that if the wise men had been wise women, they would have asked directions right from the get-go, arrived on time, helped deliver the baby, cleaned the stable, made a casserole, and brought practical gifts.

I still like the significance of the gifts of gold, frankincense, and myrrh. Gold can symbolize royalty, kingship, or divinity, the things of God (and the coin of this Child's heavenly realm are compassion, forgiveness, and peace). Frankincense with its wonderful fragrance and medicinal magic can symbolize healing (and this Child came to heal our wounds and bridge the chasm that separate us from God and one another). And myrrh or ointment can symbolize a burial embalmment (and this Child eventually through his death/resurrection made us coheirs to God's promise of eternal life).

Now there are all kinds of predictions about the war in Syria, political candidates, the Super Bowl or World Series, the Olympics, the global economy, and unpredictable and volatile nations. If you find these predictions bothersome, here's one consolation: more often than not, forecasters have been wrong.

One example: Thomas Watson, chairman of IBM, announced in 1943, "I think there is a world market for maybe five computers." Watson definitely wasn't thinking outside the box.

So I'm ignoring these and other predictions and praying this prayer:

"God, grant me the serenity to accept the things I cannot change, courage to change the things I can, and the wisdom to know the difference. Living one day at a time, enjoying one moment at a time, trusting that God will make all things right."

Today we celebrate the Epiphany, the showing forth of the child Jesus to the magi. We really don't know if they were wise men, astrologers, or spice traders. All we know is that they were non-Jews who came from far away, guided by a mysterious star and a sudden illumination of wisdom, to pay homage to this Jewish child named Jesus. Yes, Jesus is for all people.

The word of God from Isaiah takes us back to the sixth century before Jesus, when the Hebrews lost everything they thought would endure forever: Jerusalem, the temple, the monarchy. And despite this catastrophe, the author described a new Jerusalem. A divine light would emanate from this new Jerusalem and all people, Jews and non-Jews would acknowledge and walk by this light (Is 60:1–6).

Christians of course see Jesus as this light who illumines darkness, the light who shows human beings the ultimate purpose of life. Human beings are born to be in relationship with God, to manifest the glory or presence of God in their everyday attitudes and behaviors.

The letter of Paul to the Christian community at Ephesus in Turkey spoke about our future: all of us are coheirs to God's promise of eternal life, coworkers in bringing about the kingdom of God, a kingdom of truth and justice and peace and freedom (Eph 3:2–3a, 5–6).

And in the Gospel according to Matthew are all the ingredients of a great mystery novel: exotic visitors, a wicked king, court intrigue, a mysterious star, precious gifts, and a new child. The word of God became flesh so that God can transform our earthly existence into an indescribable, heavenly existence (Mt 2:1–12).

Now who is this child to whom the magi give their homage? Who is this Jesus to whom we give our ultimate allegiance as a community of faith? The early Christian community saw Jesus as the fulfillment of the hopes of ancient Israel. And so they named him the Messiah, the anointed one. The more they reflected on who he was, the more they saw Jesus not only as the fulfillment of their hopes but the foundation of their hopes.

And so they named him the eternal Word. The Gospel according to John captures this magnificently in the prologue: In the beginning was the Word, and the Word .... Yes, Jesus was the foundation as well as the fulfillment of all their hopes and our own.

This Jesus was a real historical person, flesh and blood like ourselves. He experienced, as we do, fatigue, hunger, satisfaction, joy, friendship, disappointment, loneliness, and death. He was a rabbi, a teacher, a prophet preaching that the kingdom of God was breaking into our midst.

This Jesus worked signs and wonders that proclaimed that good ultimately would triumph over evil. He possessed authority to forgive wrongdoings, and he promised eternal life. He had a unique relationship with the God of ancient Israel; in fact, he was one with God, but he was crucified and then raised up from the dead, transfigured into a new heavenly reality. He is alive in our midst today, especially in the sacramental life of the Christian community. And because he is alive, we too are alive with God's grace and favor.

Jesus taught not only that the kingdom of God was breaking into our midst but also that you and I can share in this kingdom of God by living out a life of discipleship. And how is that? By living prayerfully in the presence of God; by recognizing that our lives do have an ultimate purpose; by seeing in Jesus the Word made flesh, the face of God; by reaching out compassionately with a helping hand to the people around us; by experiencing the presence of the living Christ, body and blood, soul and divinity, sacramentally and mystically in liturgy; and by always being ready to let go of our earthly life, in the mystery of death, so that we can be in relationship with God forever. Yes, in death is the hope of eternal life.

Jesus also taught that God is our Father, a compassionate God, always near us at the start of each day to guide us on our journey to our heavenly home.

So, on this the Feast of the Epiphany or manifestation of the presence of God, I invite all of us to rededicate ourselves to Jesus Christ and to ask him to grace us anew at the beginning of this new year, so that we might grow ever more deeply in our relationship with God and manifest ever more clearly the glory of God in our everyday attitudes and behaviors.

I conclude with a favorite New Year message, worth repeating:

The most destructive habit	Worry
The greatest joy	Giving
The greatest loss	Loss of self-respect
The most satisfying work	Helping others
The ugliest personality trait	Selfishness
The most endangered species	Dedicated leaders
Our greatest natural resource	Our young people
The greatest shot in the arm	Encouragement
The greatest problem to overcome	Fear
The most effective sleeping pill	Peace of mind
The most crippling failure disease	Excuses
The most powerful force in life	Love
The most dangerous pariah	A gossiper
The world's most incredible computer	The brain
The worst thing to be without	Hope
The deadliest weapon	The tongue
The two most power-filled words	"I Can"
The greatest asset	Faith
The most worthless emotion	Self-pity
The most beautiful attire	A smile
The most prized possession	Integrity
The most powerful channel of communication	Prayer
The most contagious spirit	Enthusiasm

Truly something to live by, manifesting the glory of God in our everyday attitudes and behaviors.

THE BAPTISM OF THE LORD

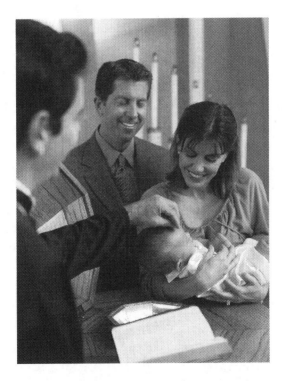

The image of water reminds me of the fire-and-brimstone preacher who railed against the evils of drinking. He bellowed, "If I had all the beer in the world, I'd pour it into the river." Then he shouted, "If I had all the wine in the world, I'd pour it into the river." And finally, he thundered, "I'd pour all the whiskey into the river." The song leader burst out singing "Shall we Gather at the River."

I notice more and more people have tattoos. Colorful geometric designs, flowers, crosses, and so on. Tattoos and brands were often chosen as a mark of identity. And anyone thinking about getting a tattoo should really want it forever. Getting rid of a tattoo is not so easy. Indelible, identity—these are key aspects of what it means to be marked or tattooed.

In baptism, we have been branded, so to speak—identified by God as belonging to a community of disciples. Yet baptism is not a simple tattoo or rite or milestone; it is a transformative experience in which God lives in us and we live in God within a grace-filled community. That's our indelible identity. We become empowered by God's grace, God's favor, to live as a community of disciples.

Today we celebrate the baptism of Jesus by John in the Jordan River. And in this celebratory event, our Catholic community invites all of us to renew our own baptismal promises so that we can live ever more transparently as disciples of Jesus, trying to do, as best we can, what's the right thing.

The word of God takes us back in our imaginations to the sixth century before Jesus (the 500s) to the Hebrew exile in ancient Babylonia (what we know today as modern Iraq). God spoke to Isaiah: "Comfort my people. You are about to be liberated from your oppressors in Babylonia." "Prepare the way of the Lord," Isaiah shouted, "for your triumphant God to reenter Jerusalem. And let all people see the glory of God" (Is 40:1–5, 9–11).

The author challenges us to ask whether we let God into our own lives, whether we are other-centered, God and people-centered, and not self-centered. And do our everyday attitudes and behaviors reflect the glory or presence of God?

The pastoral letter to Titus illuminated the glory of God in Jesus, who reestablished our relationship with God so that we can live godly lives, always eager to do the right thing. Through baptism, God's Spirit has been richly poured out upon us so that we might live a life of virtue: self-discipline, compassion, responsibility, courage, friendship, honesty, loyalty, faith in God (Ti 2:11–14; 3:4–7). The author may be asking whether we are indeed living a godly life, a Spirit-filled life as befits heirs to God's promise of eternal life.

In the Gospel according to Mark, John baptized his cousin, Jesus, in the Jordan River. And as Jesus came up out of the waters, the Spirit or power or energy of God overwhelmed him. He is indeed God's "beloved Son" (Mark 1:11) anointed to carry out his Messianic mission, drawing human beings into a filial relationship with God.

Now, John the Baptist was an interesting personality in the Gospels. He dressed simply and ate locusts and wild honey. But what was his vocation or calling? To point to Jesus as the Messiah. As we reflect upon John's vocation, we might ask, by virtue of who we are and what we do, whether we reflect Jesus Christ in our relationships with one another. And what is John doing? He is baptizing, inviting people to turn their lives around, to turn toward God and away from self-centeredness.

Baptism is a rite of initiation into a community of disciples. In early Christianity, candidates, more often than not, were immersed in water. Water symbolizes life and death. It can be life-giving (when we're dehydrated) or death threatening (a hurricane). When the candidate stepped into the pool of water and came up on the other side, he/she symbolized in that gesture a dying to self-centeredness and a rising to a God-centered life. By the eleventh century, baptism by immersion became the exception, and baptism by pouring water over the head of the candidate became the common practice.

Why be baptized? To answer the question, we first have to understand who we are in relationship to God. The book of Genesis captures this graphically. In the beginning, Genesis says, man and woman walked with God; they had friendship with God and friendship with one another. But somehow they lost that relationship. Genesis describes very simply yet very powerfully their fall. They hid from God, man blamed woman, and even the earthly elements began to work against them. But human beings forever cry out for ultimate purpose, relationship with God. That is why God became flesh in Jesus. Jesus, through his horrible death and glorious resurrection, reestablished that relationship.

Thus, baptism initiates us into a community of disciples who have a relationship with God.

This new relationship makes very straight-forward demands, summed

31

up in the so-called Ten Commandments, really statements about freedom from attitudes and behaviors that undermine our relationship with God and one another.

The Ten Commandments say very simply that our God is a God of love, and our response to God's unconditional love is gratitude. And this planet of ours, and the people on it reflect the image of our God. And so all of creation—human beings in particular—is worthy of reverence. God deserves our time, and that's why we take time to grow in that relationship with God. This same God challenges us to support virtues—for example, caring for aging parents; cherishing life from beginning to end; being faithful to our promises; respecting the rights of others; speaking the truth; not exploiting people or treating them as objects; and being generous rather than greedy with what we have.

The Ten Commandments underscore virtues we should practice every day.

And so today, as we reflect upon the baptism of Jesus, and as we enjoy the waters outside our parish church, I invite us to renew our own baptismal promises, to live godly lives as sons or daughters of God our Father.

Someone wrote that "you and I are writing our own gospel, a chapter each day, by the deeds we do, by the words we say." Pray for the grace to write your own living gospel so that others will recognize in you the glory or presence of God. And so today, we ought to give thanks to God for this global faith community to which we belong, a community that calls us into a relationship with God here and now and forever in a life beyond this earthly life.

Second Sunday in Ordinary Time

D id you notice anything different in church today? The Christmas crèche is back in storage. The poinsettias are gone. We are now in "Ordinary time." The color of the chasuble is green, not white.

Let me begin with a brief story. A hospital got a call from an elderly woman who said, "I'd like information about a patient. All the information, A to Z." The hospital receptionist replied, "Would you please hold?" Then a very authoritative-sounding voice came on the phone and said, "You are calling about one of our patients?" She said, "Yes, I need all the information about Mary Smith in room 610."

Unthinking, he said, "Let me bring up her file … Okay … Mary Smith is doing well. Her doctor notes that if she continues improving, he will release her from the hospital next Thursday." The woman said, "Thank God! I'm so happy to hear that." The fellow asked, "I take it you're one of Mary Smith's family members." She said, "I *am* Mary Smith! I'm calling from my hospital bed. No one tells me anything, so I called the operator." So much for communication channels.

The word of God takes us back in our imaginations to the sixth century before Jesus (the 500s) to the city of Jerusalem. Ancient Babylonia had reduced Jerusalem to rubble.

Today we know certain cities by nicknames. New York is the Big Apple; Chicago is the Windy City; Paris is the City of Lights. Jerusalem was once known as the City of Lights because it was on a hill illuminated with torches during Jewish festivals. The author described Jerusalem as "desolate" and "forsaken." But one day, the author wrote, in the

33

not-so-distant future, Jerusalem will rise up out of its ashes, and God will again delight in Jerusalem and its people. Yes, God will turn Israel's tragic history into a glorious future (Is 62:1–5).

The author may ask us, "Does God delight in us?" In other words, do we reveal the glory or presence of God in our everyday attitudes and behaviors?

Paul, in his letter to the Christian community at Corinth, noted the many gifts we have. All these gifts are meant for the common good, for building up the community. Yes, people working together can perform extraordinary deeds (1 Cor 12:4–11).

Together, we can spark each other's imagination and creativity, encourage and motivate one another, magnify each other's efforts and abilities—and that is why people working together can accomplish so much more than individuals.

For example, occasionally when I enter an airplane, I think about the hundreds of people who take care of it: pilots and flight attendants, schedulers, weather staff, cleaning people, mechanics, marketers advertising discount fares, dispatchers planning routes, controllers watching radar screens, FAA inspectors ensuring safety, manufacturers tracking the quality of the planes, engineers testing wingspans, and the many other people who concentrate on making passengers' journeys safe. An airplane requires teamwork. So too does our global Catholic community. And our legislators might benefit from Paul's advice to seek the common good in their deliberations.

In the Gospel according to John, the author began the so-called Book of Signs: seven signs Jesus works that reveal his true identity. Jesus is indeed one with God; in fact, he is God. This first sign Jesus worked in the town of Cana in the region of Galilee (Jn 2:1–11).

Now there are different levels of meaning in this story, as in so many Gospel stories. On one level, Jesus, his mother, and the disciples have simply been invited to a local wedding. Mary, in some ways, could pass for a wedding planner. And there's an embarrassing shortage of wine. Mary may have even said to the waiters something like, "See that handsome man there? That's my son. Do whatever he says."

On another level, Mary appears as our mediator, interceding with her Son on our behalf. And that is why our Catholic Christian heritage gives a special place of honor to Mary. On a third level, the water made wine symbolizes the breaking in of the kingdom of God—the symbolic wedding banquet at the end of time with fine wines and delicious food. And on a fourth level, this first sign is one of seven in which the author points to Jesus as "the revelation" of God to us.

The point is there can be many levels of meaning in scripture.

In light of the wedding at Cana, I would like to reflect briefly upon the sacrament of marriage. Now there are all kinds of literature about relationships, self-improvement, and so on.

Often people are looking for the perfect this or that and forget that life is not perfect and often we have to muddle through things and simply do the best we can. In fact, I doubt there's such a thing as the perfect marriage. Marriages can be described in three stages: the honeymoon; disillusionment (i.e., he/she is not exactly the person I initially thought); and then the third stage, where the partnership becomes a friendship. They become best friends. They have vowed to be true to each other, to honor each other. Their friendship is indeed a covenant where they live for each other, live for God, and live for others (e.g., their children). And that is true love.

True love can emerge only if we forgive, work out compromises (in other words, be flexible), disagree without being disagreeable, compliment each other regularly, look for the good (we all have warts), clarify our essential or core values, accept differences (our way isn't the only way), seek a balance between how much is enough and how much is too much (for example, a tightwad/spendthrift combo is a challenge), and communicate regularly. Don't let the care of children trump our primary vocation, which is to love one another. And try to find the balance between work, family, and personal time.

As an aside, when sorting through a slight, remember to always distinguish between behavior and negative judgments about that behavior—for example, *you're late for the birthday party* (behavior) versus *you're the most inconsiderate person I know* (negative judgment). Maybe there was an accident on the highway or something else. Always focus on the behavior and avoid negative judgments about the behavior.

As with most things in life, we must work at good relationships— sticking together, especially through rough patches, with the confidence that times will change and we'll reemerge closer. I like the prayer that says live one day at a time; enjoy one moment at a time; trust that God will make all things right if I try, as best I can, to do what is right and true and fair."

Above all, make room for God in our relationships.

And so the wedding of Cana invites all of us, and especially husbands and wives, to reflect upon our relationships. Married couples especially might ask, "How can I keep that original glow alive? Yes, with the friend for whom I live, the friend with whom I laugh, the friend I love above all else on earth, how can we continue to cherish and support and reenergize that relationship?"

THIRD SUNDAY IN ORDINARY TIME

A controversial fire-and-brimstone preacher created one crisis after another. Finally, his bishop decided to transfer him. The preacher, announcing the transfer from his pulpit, said: "The same Jesus who led me to this parish is now leading me to another." When the preacher finished, the music leader called out, "'What a Friend We Have in Jesus.'" Thank God for friends.

The word of God takes us back to the fifth century before Jesus (the 400s), to a Jewish religious leader by the name of Ezra. It was a time of new beginnings for the Jews who returned to the ruins of Jerusalem decades after ancient Babylonia reduced the city to rubble. The Jews were rebuilding their lives, much like many Europeans did in the aftermath of WWII. Ezra gathered the people together, men, women, and children, in a liturgical assembly to renew the covenant God had made with them centuries before on Mount Sinai—a covenant summed up in a single phrase: "You are my people; and I am your God." The people who heard Ezra cried out, "Amen. Amen." So be it. They will not only be hearers of God's word but doers of that word as well (Neh 8:2–4a, 5–6, 8–10).

This covenantal renewal challenges us to renew our own baptismal promises: to live an other-centered life with God and for others.

Paul, in his letter to the Christian community at Corinth in Greece, addressed all kinds of problems: doctrinal squabbles, moral misconduct, personality problems, and cliques, each with its own hero (1 Cor 12:12–30). Paul used the metaphor of the human body to describe how the different parts—the eye, the ear, the voice, the hands, the feet—have different functions, yet they all work for the good of the whole body (1 Cor 12:12–26).

St. Paul championed unity within diversity. We are one family, brothers and sisters to one another and sons and daughters of God. God lives within us, and we live in God within a grace-filled community. And how appropriate that we, in the week of prayer for Christian unity, should pray, like Paul centuries ago, that the Spirit will make all Christians one, for together we profess that there is only one Lord, one faith, and one baptism.

In the Gospel according to Luke, Jesus began his public ministry, his mission. He went back to his hometown of Nazareth in the region of Galilee and walked into the local synagogue on the Sabbath, and from the parchment of scripture—in particular, the book of the prophet Isaiah—he read from that magnificent passage about the jubilee year: "The Spirit of the Lord is upon me … he has sent me to bring glad tidings …." Concluding, Jesus rolled up the scroll and said, "Today this scripture passage is fulfilled in your hearing" (Luke 1:1–4; 4:14–21).

This was indeed a bold and shocking statement for the synagogue audience. In a real sense, this was the inaugural speech of Jesus as he started his public ministry, proclaiming aloud freedom from what enslaves us, vision from what blinds us, and healing from what breaks relationships. Jesus then set about giving hope to those who have lost hope, purpose in life to those who have found little or no meaning in life.

Yes, Jesus challenges us to forgive one another, to seek reconciliation in our relationships, to live an other-centered life, not a self-centered one, and to seek first the kingdom of God. This is the program Jesus proclaimed at the beginning of his ministry.

The word of God provides us with many themes upon which to meditate, but I would like to illuminate a single line from the book of the prophet Isaiah: "The Spirit of the Lord is upon me … and He has sent me to bring glad tidings." Yes, the Spirit of the Lord is also upon all of us, you and me, to bring good news (Jesus Christ, risen and alive) to our families, workplaces, communities, our fellow human beings.

Let me tell you about someone who brought good news.

One of the poorest neighborhoods in our country is a twenty-minute subway ride from Wall Street. This South Bronx neighborhood was plagued with poverty, homelessness, AIDS, and crack-cocaine and heroin addiction. Children struggled to grow up in houses that were iceboxes in winter and fire traps infested with vermin in the summer.

Author, educator, and social activist Jonathan Kozol chronicled stories of these people in two best-selling books, *Amazing Grace: The Lives of Children* and *Conscience of a Nation* and *Ordinary Resurrections: Children in the Years of Hope*. Despite the miseries, Kozol found hope, because a little Episcopal church—St. Ann's—ran a thriving after-school program for children, an evening recovery program for adults, a food bank, a Sunday soup kitchen more like a family dinner, and a 24/7 approach to all kinds of emergencies. Yes, despite their struggles, people experienced a dignity and generosity that made the parish an authentic family of faith in God.

One of Kozol's heroes was a woman named Martha Overall. When people were sick, she took them to the hospital. When children were arrested, she went to court. She was there for baptisms and burials. She took on building managers, loan sharks, drug dealers, and city bureaucracy. She did everything from offering prayers to making sandwiches to mopping the church floor. For Kozol, she proclaimed the good news, especially to the poor.

As disciples of Jesus, we too are called to proclaim the good news. Just as St. Ann's became a sanctuary for people in the South Bronx, so too we are called to create a sanctuary in our families, workplaces, and community, a place where fellow human beings can find faith in God, hope in the future, friendship and peace, and support in life's problems.

We might ask ourselves as we enter the new year, "How can I be a better person in bringing good news to others?" I like this simple suggestion: each day, do a little bit more than you think you can. Love a little bit more; forgive a little bit more; reach out to someone who is hurting; sacrifice a little bit more with our time and talent; encourage one another, especially our families, a bit more.

And you know what? God will give us that power of the Spirit, that same Spirit that descended upon Jesus, to do a bit more than we think we can. If we do a little bit more each day, then when our earthly life ends, we will approach God a little bit closer than we thought we could.

FOURTH SUNDAY IN ORDINARY TIME

I rediscovered a book, *Disorder in the American Courts*, which quotes things people actually said in court. For example, an attorney asked: "How was your first marriage terminated?" The witness replied, "By death." The attorney continued, "By whose death?" The witness said, "Take a guess."

In another case, an attorney said, "Describe the individual." The witness replied, "He was about medium height and had a beard." The attorney: "Was it a male or a female?" The witness said, "Unless the circus was in town, I'm going with male."

And finally this: "Do you recall the time that you examined the body?" Reply: "The autopsy started around 8 p.m." Attorney: "And Mr. McGoo, was he dead at the time?" Witness: "If not, he was by the time I finished the autopsy."

Court stenographers actually recorded these statements. Hilarious reading.

The word of God takes us back in our imaginations over six centuries before Jesus, traumatic times for ancient Israel. The Hebrews lost their kingdom, their king, their city of Jerusalem, and their temple. In this passage, God called Jeremiah to be a prophet, to speak on behalf of God. Jeremiah described how the Hebrews were unfaithful to their covenantal promises; then he proclaimed a new covenant and urged the Hebrews not to fight against the Babylonians but to surrender. How unpatriotic and outrageous of Jeremiah to say this, many thought. And for this especially, he encountered all kinds of opposition. And yet, because

Jeremiah believed God was with him, he continued to speak God's message courageously (Jer 1:4–5, 17–19).

The author may be asking us whether we stand up for what's right, or do we simply go along to get along.

Paul, in his letter to the Christian community in Corinth, poetically described in an ode or hymn the many facets love. Love, Paul wrote, is not showy gifts like "speaking in tongues or uttering prophecies." It is not envious or rude or irritable. Nor does it insist "on its own way." No, love is like a prism that reflects myriad characteristics of love: patience, kindness, generosity, faithfulness, forgiveness, compassion, self-discipline, peace, joy. Above all, love never ceases because God is love. Love is eternity in God's presence (1 Cor 12:31—13:13).

Paul may be asking us whether we practice these characteristics of love.

In the Gospel according to Luke, the author highlighted how Jesus, like Jeremiah and Paul, pursued his mission uncompromisingly. He proclaimed that the kingdom of God was breaking into our midst, that all people can share in this kingdom by living a life of discipleship, a life of virtue. That God would include non-Jews shocked some in the synagogue. In fact, it outraged them (Lk 4:21–30).

Like Jeremiah and Paul, Jesus encountered opposition even from his own townspeople. And yet, because God was with him, Jesus continued, whatever the consequences. Jeremiah, Paul, and Jesus had one passion in life: to speak of God. That mission fired them up.

The question for us is, what energizes us? Where do we find purpose in our lives? Some argue convincingly that we find meaning in a mix of what we do, what we experience, and our attitude toward our own inescapable suffering and dying.

Let me give you a true example. A newly minted medical doctor found purpose primarily in his work as a physician. But he discovered he had inoperable spinal cancer, which gradually paralyzed him. Soon he couldn't work. So, what did he do? He began to find meaning primarily in his everyday experiences, especially at the facility where he was cared for. He spoke with other patients, entertained and encouraged them. He read good books, listened to music, stayed in touch with faraway family.

But at length, he couldn't even do these things. His life took another turn. This young doctor now had to find meaning primarily in his own inescapable suffering and dying. What did he do? He became a counselor to fellow sufferers and an example by bearing his own suffering bravely, not complaining. Finally, he had to let go of his own life, and in doing so, with faith in God, he made a leap into the mystery of death and into the hands of God, much like a trapeze artist who lets go of that rope, trusting that his fellow artist will catch him in that free fall.

Life indeed was worth living to the end. This physician found meaning in every stage. In the medical profession. In his experiences. And eventually in his suffering and dying.

This raises the question, what are human beings meant for? Or, put another way, what is our life on this planet all about? Most of our finest thinkers have held that we are meant for something greater than merely eating and sleeping. Yes, we are meant for something far beyond mere animal instincts, beyond acquiring and spending, beyond having a nice home, a fancy car, a vacation getaway, beyond all the scientific achievements, engineering marvels, and economic feats of this world.

What is that "something?" The answer points to something transcendent, beyond ourselves: the human spirit. Always open to a relationship with an awesome God and to one another. Yes, our purpose, no matter our profession or age, is to be in relationship with God and one another forever.

Staying on message, I would like to conclude briefly with another true story that captures the courage of Jeremiah, Paul, and Jesus. A nineteen-year-old student at Harvard in the late 1960s, Kent Keith, wrote what he called the "Paradoxical Commandments." He published them without much notice and then moved on with his life. But in the age of the Internet, someone transmitted the "Paradoxical Commandments," which began circling the globe, attributed to everyone from psychiatrist Karl Menninger to Mother Teresa (they were seen on the wall of her home for children in Calcutta). It was a paradox when it was discovered they were written by a student no one heard of. Here they are:

> People are illogical, unreasonable, and self-centered;
> Love them anyway.
> If you do good, people will accuse you of selfish, ulterior
> motives; Do good anyway.

If you are successful, you win false friends and true enemies; Succeed anyway.

The good you do today will be forgotten tomorrow; Do good anyway.

Honesty and frankness make you vulnerable; Be honest and frank anyway.

The biggest men and women with the biggest ideas can be shot down by the smallest men and women with the smallest minds; Think big anyway.

People favor underdogs, but follow only top dogs; Fight for the underdogs anyway.

What you spend years building may be destroyed in one night; Build anyway.

People really need help but may attack you if you do help them; Help people anyway.

And finally give the world the best you have and you'll get kicked in the teeth;

Give the world the best you have anyway.

Something to think about and something to do in light of the three personalities in today's word of God: Jeremiah, Paul, and Jesus.

FIFTH SUNDAY IN ORDINARY TIME

A quick survey: how many will be watching the Super Bowl? How many think there is too much sports on TV? Whatever, many will be happy when the Super Bowl is over. In the meantime, I urge those who don't like football to be patient with those who do. If you are a casual watcher, you might follow the advice of Andy Rooney: find something about one of the teams you don't like and cheer for the other team. For example, you don't like the color of the uniforms, or you had a bad hotel room in Denver or Charlotte. This will make the Super Bowl more interesting for you.

The word of God takes us back in our imaginations to the eighth century before Jesus (the 700s) to a man named Isaiah who has an awesome experience of God in the Jerusalem temple. The temple shook with the thunderous acclamation of angelic creatures, and Isaiah was awestruck. Then an angel cleansed him with God's mercy (Is 6:1–2a, 3–8).

God then commissioned Isaiah, filled with God's grace, to become a prophet, to speak on God's behalf to the Hebrews. Although they had forgotten their covenantal promises, God had not forgotten his, summed up in that simple yet profound statement, "You are my people, and I am your God." Isaiah challenges us to remember that God has called us to be faithful to our baptismal promises, to live a life worthy of our calling.

Paul, in his letter to the Christian community, emphasized his one passion in life: to preach Jesus once crucified and now risen and alive among us. Paul wrote that he too was called to be an apostle on the road to Damascus in Syria, and that experience of the living Christ turned

Paul's life upside down. God's grace, Paul proclaimed, made him what he is. And God's grace, which we should pray for every day, can make us passionate about witnessing to our faith, about proclaiming God's good news: Jesus is alive and calls us into relationship with him forever (1 Cor 15:1–11).

In the Gospel according to Luke, Jesus went into the deep waters of the Sea of Galilee with Peter and the other fishermen. Peter, while skeptical about fishing again after catching nothing all night, recognized something special in Jesus. So Peter cast the nets again and made a sensational catch. Suddenly Peter experienced the awesome presence of God in Jesus. He cried out, "Lord." And then Jesus, the master, calmed them, "Do not be afraid," and called Peter and the others into discipleship. And how did they respond? They left everything they had and followed Jesus (Luke 5:1–11).

These three biblical personalities—Isaiah, Paul, and Jesus—accomplished much because they loved much; they were on fire with an intense love of God and a compassionate love of their fellow human beings with a message of hope in the future. Theirs was a purpose-driven life, to quote Rick Warren's best seller. And they fired people up with God's grace so that they were able to choose their better selves, give their time and talent for the furtherance of God's kingdom of truth and justice and freedom and peace, and stand up for what was right.

Jesus, the master, has also called us to a life of discipleship through the life-giving waters of baptism. Now what is baptism?

To begin with, baptism is God's gift to you and me. And our basic response to God's gift is gratitude. Gratitude that we are alive, gratitude that we are who we are. Baptism is a mystery that defines us, marks us, and transforms us at the very core of our being. Baptism shapes who we are and how we try to live.

Baptism, in other words, means christened. We are plunged into the mystery of Jesus Christ. St. Paul captured this magnificently when he wrote to the Christian community in Galatia: "Christ lives in me." Christening describes how I live: struggling to follow Jesus, the God-man, the primary sacrament of seven, the flesh-and-blood visible sign of God's grace. Jesus is indeed the face of God.

Yes, God has made us "new creatures." The living Christ is our exemplar or blueprint.

In fact, the universe reflects the presence of God in myriad forms. And baptized and confirmed in the Spirit, we celebrate the mystery of the death and resurrection of Jesus Christ at the table of the Lord. This celebration sends us out among others to live our baptismal and Eucharistic mission: to live a Godlike life, to live in a manner worthy of our calling, to treat all God's creatures with respect—especially human beings, for humans are made in the image of God.

What precisely does "sent out to others" mean?

Every one of us has gifts or talents that can empower or build up other people. Football's Peyton Manning or celebrities like Meryl Streep or Denzel Washington are not the only people with gifts or talents. You and I have special gifts and talents as well, by virtue of our baptism. We possess the power to believe, to hope, and to love. And within our common Christian life, there are many splendid callings.

I love the image of "a thousand points of light." God shines with transcendent brilliance. And those who ask for the grace to draw closer to God glow with that radiance. They become one of those points of light. Teacher or student, businessman or businesswoman, whoever you are, you have a specific vocation/calling to fire up people with God's grace so that they will choose their better selves, give their time and talents to others, and stand up for what is right, by simply being an example. We are called to become one of those thousand points of light.

Yes, God has given all of us gifts. Let us rejoice as the Virgin Mary rejoiced. Yes, always look for the good in ourselves, in others, and in the situations in life. And then we will truly, with God's grace, realize our authentic potential as sons and daughters of God our Father.

I close with a prayerful thought that sums up the search for our authentic self:

> Fortunate are the persons, who in this life can find,
> a purpose that can fill their days and goals to fill their mind.
> For in this world there is a need for those who'll lead the rest,
> to rise above the "average" life, by giving of their best!

Will you be one, who dares to try when challenged by the task, to rise to heights you've never seen, or is that too much to ask?

May we all realize that, in the end, the purpose of our baptismal calling is to matter, to count, to make a difference for the better by giving the best we have in service to one another! And then we will realize with God's grace our authentic selves.

First Sunday of Lent

You may have heard about a husband, always the listener, and a wife, always the talker. One day, they went for a drive. Suddenly a policeman pulled up and said, "Do you know that your wife fell out a mile back?" The husband said, "Oh, thank God. I thought I was going deaf." So much for listening skills.

Wednesday, we began our Lenten journey to Easter. The word "Lent" comes from an Anglo-Saxon word meaning spring. Yes, Lent symbolizes the renewal of our spiritual life. The point of Lent is often people pursue purpose in such things as wealth, power, and celebrity. In the process, they forget the things that truly matter—our relationships with God and one another.

I think of a true story. The father was a common laborer, the mother chronically ill. Life was a succession of small apartments, simple food, and hand-me-downs. Their son wanted to escape this. By age forty, he realized the so-called American dream: a partnership with an investment firm, a beautiful home, a loving family, and more than enough money.

Then his father died. And looking through his father's memorabilia, the son discovered a letter written in his father's hand, dated years before. The letter read:

Hi, Johnny.

I'm your daddy. I've waited so long to say that. The doctors told your mom and me we could never have a child of our own. But every day we prayed for a miracle.

And then, much to everyone's surprise, you were born: our miracle child. Johnny, to be your daddy means picking you up when you fall and holding you when you are afraid. Being your daddy means loving you just because you are my son, the best part of who I am.

There's so much in my heart, so many dreams for you. You have brought joy into our lives, a joy that your mom and I thought we'd never know ... Son, I'll never be rich. But I believe that when God helped us find our way to you, God also would be "beside us" the rest of our lives. We would always have each other, and that's more than I ever hoped for. Just keep in mind who you are, where you've come from, and how much we love you, our miracle child.

It was only then that the son realized what mattered in life.

Lent challenges us to refocus ourselves on what truly matters—our relationships with God and one another—and to have a change of heart, to become more aware of God's presence in our daily lives, and to pay more attention to the needs of others.

The word of God in the book of Deuteronomy, chapter 26, carries us back in our imaginations to the early history of ancient Israel. The author focuses on identity. Who are you? What are your roots? Sometimes we pursue that question through genealogy or DNA. The author reminded the Hebrews of their roots: once at-risk Syrians; exploited as cheap labor in Egypt; brought to a place of abundance; and now grateful to the God who saved you. The author may be asking us, do we know our Christian identity? In baptism, we were branded and transformed into a "new creature." We were christened, plunged into the mystery of Jesus Christ. Christ now lives in us, and we live in Christ. That's our spiritual identity.

Paul, in his letter to the Christian community in Rome, proclaimed fundamental truths: Jesus is our Lord to whom we owe our allegiance; God raised up Jesus from the dead; Jesus Christ lives; and because he lives, we live. And through the gift of faith, we have salvation, eternal life (Rom 10:8–13).

In the Gospel according to Luke, chapter 4, Jesus was tempted in the wilderness as the Hebrews were tested centuries before. But where the Hebrews failed, Jesus succeeds. The devil appears, not as a guy with a pitchfork but as a seductive voice, tempting Jesus to use his wonder-working powers to satisfy his hunger. But Jesus's food is God's word, not bread alone. Then the devil offers Jesus earthly power and prestige if he will only worship him. But Jesus belongs to God's kingdom. To God alone belongs worship. Finally, the devil asks Jesus to do a daring performance that will make him famous. But Jesus refuses to test God by presuming upon such a spectacular display. To God alone belongs praise and honor.

In some form or other, these are temptations that many human beings face: seeking only pleasure (or self-indulgence), pursuing power unscrupulously, or craving fame insatiably (with spectacular displays or feats). Jesus will have none of these things. He will remain true to his identity and vocation. He will serve God alone and only do the will of his heavenly Father. The author may be asking us how true we are to our spiritual identity as baptized Christians.

Our Christian Lenten discipline focuses on the way to be true to our identity: prayer, fasting, and almsgiving. Lent challenges us to rediscover and retreat ourselves to these age-old disciplines.

1. Retreat ourselves to prayer. Prayer is an awareness of our absolute dependency upon God, a grateful response to God for our ever-so-brief lives. Prayer simply brings to consciousness the presence of God that is already around us and within us. Now there are many approaches to prayer: familiar prayers like the Our Father, this liturgy, the prayer of silence or petition. All of these approaches are simply pathways into the presence of God. How often and how well do we pray? Even now, am I entering as fully as possible into this liturgy by participating wholeheartedly in the singing, listening attentively as God speaks to us in scripture?

2. Second, retreat ourselves to fasting. Fasting is a Gospel value but not fasting alone. Fasting and almsgiving are Gospel twins. For the early Christians, going without food "enabled the hungry to eat." But fasting is more than doing without food. Our Lenten

fast can mean doing without other things as well. Doing without anger, impatience, self-centeredness, negative judgments about others, or whatever prevents us from living the Gospel message of love.

3. And finally, retreat ourselves to almsgiving. In early Christianity, there were no government agencies providing assistance to the poor, the needy, the homeless, the underprivileged, and the sick. Alms-giving was seen as an essential addition to prayer and fasting, not only during Lent but every day. Share what we have with others and for others. Share our time; visit, listen, write. Share our talent. Share our money with needy people, if we can. Share ourselves; smile more often to let others know that you want them to share your joy.

Yes, as we begin the Lenten season, it's time for a change of heart, to become more aware of God's presence in our lives. I invite all of us to rediscover and retreat ourselves to prayer, fasting, and care for others, so we can refocus on what truly matters—our relationships with God and one another.

SECOND SUNDAY OF LENT

How many have visited the Whitney Museum on Fifth Avenue in Manhattan? I was there a while ago, standing before a large gold frame and lamenting the sorry state of modern art. I said to the docent, whom I knew, "This portrait is a monstrosity." And the docent said, "You're looking at a mirror."

I want to share a story about Montgomery, Alabama, in 1955. Some of you know the story well. Black people sitting anywhere in a bus were expected to give up their seat to a white person.

Rosa Parks, a forty-two-year-old seamstress, was riding home after a very hard day's work. White people got on the bus, and the driver asked African Americans to move to the back. Rosa refused. The bus driver called the police, and she was arrested and jailed for violating the segregation law. Looking back, she noted that she had always been a timid person, but "my entire life demanded of me that I be courageous," to stand up for what was the right thing.

The boycott of the buses began. Rosa lost her job. Threats were made to kill her. But she was not easily frightened. She stood her ground. That single audacious act transformed her into a new person and gave rise to the civil rights movement of the sixties that forced a nation to confront racial inequality.

One lesson from the true story is this: each one of us possesses within ourselves the Spirit of God by virtue of the life-giving waters of baptism, and that Spirit of God empowers us to become transformational agents of change for the better among our fellow human beings.

In fact, Jesus Christ challenges all of us—his fellow coworkers—to become transformational agents of change for the better. We, as coworkers with God, have to do our best to transform unfairness and prejudice into fairness; transform hate into peace; indifference into compassion; sorrow into joy; despair into hope.

Yes, we have to work to transform self-centeredness into other-centeredness, God-centeredness, and loneliness into family or community. And one way to do this in our homes, workplaces, parishes, or neighborhoods is doing all the good we can, in all the ways we can, in all the places we can, at all the times we can, for all the people we can, as long as ever we can.

Now the word of God takes us back almost four thousand years to the land that we know today as Iraq. In Genesis, chapter 15, Abraham hears the call of God. And because he was a man of faith who trusted completely in God, he set out for an unknown land. Now many of us can relate to this challenge. Going off to college? Or to a new job? Or to another part of the country? You didn't quite know how things would go. You may have been anxious, afraid. I'm sure Abraham was anxious. And yet because Abraham trusted completely in God, God made a covenant with him and promised Abraham children and land and prosperity. And God calls you and me to be people of faith, to trust completely in God in spite of all the challenges we meet in our daily lives.

Paul, in his letter to the Christian community in Philippi in Greece, proclaims that our citizenship is in heaven. And yes, God will change our fragile human selves into glorified selves. So stand firm in your faith. God calls you and me to a life beyond this earthly life. We are citizens of heaven. And so Paul urges us to live lives worthy of our calling now so that we share in a glorious future later.

In the Gospel according to Luke, the disciples experienced the transfiguration of Jesus; they saw the unique and awesome presence of God in Jesus of Nazareth. And as the scriptures describe this experience, the face of Jesus became as dazzling as the sun, his clothes as "white as light," an allusion to the white cloth given us at baptism. The disciples suddenly saw a vision of the "glorious" Jesus beyond the flesh and blood Jesus of their everyday life. They saw the face of God in their midst, the Father's beloved Son (Lk 9:28–36).

But who is this Jesus, the face of God in our midst? The early Christian community saw Jesus as the fulfillment of all their hopes, and so they named him the Messiah or anointed one. And the more they reflected on who he was, the more they saw him not only as the fulfillment but as the foundation of their hopes as well, and so they also named him the Word, the eternal Word that the prologue to the Gospel according to John captures so magnificently in the passage, "In the beginning was the Word ..."

The Jesus of the Gospels is not the Jesus of Dan Brown's *The Da Vinci Code*, which is more fiction than fact. Jesus was a real historical person like ourselves. He experienced fatigue, hunger, joy, friendship, disappointment, and loneliness as we do. But he was more than a man. He had a unique relationship to the God of ancient Israel; he was one with God. He was a rabbi, a teacher, a prophet who proclaimed the kingdom of God was breaking into our midst. He worked signs and wonders, healings and exorcisms, which heralded the ultimate triumph of good over evil, of life over death. And through his own life, death, and resurrection, he opened to us the doors of eternal life with God.

And what did Jesus teach? That the kingdom of God was breaking into our midst and that you and I can share in this kingdom by living a life of discipleship with Jesus here and now: a life of regular prayer; a life of fasting or giving up those attitudes and behaviors that can break or fracture not only our relationship with God but also our relationships with one another; and a life of almsgiving or generous volunteer service to one another. And thirdly, he taught that God is our Father. And this is indeed a tremendous reality of our faith. The God of this magnificent universe, our creator who became flesh in Jesus and is alive in our midst by the power of the Spirit—yes, the triune God lives and dwells within us.

And so today as we reexperience the call to travel into the unknown, and as we reflect upon our citizenship in heaven, and in particular as we meditate upon the vision of Jesus that the disciples experienced, may the word of God inspire us to renew ourselves spiritually and to rededicate ourselves to Jesus the Christ in regular prayer to God, to give up attitudes and behaviors that can break or fracture not only our relationship with God but also our relationship with one another, and to live a life in generous volunteer service so that we participate fully in the kingdom of God—gloriously alive with the glorious Christ.

Third Sunday of Lent

S ome of you may know that I spent most of my priestly ministry in higher education. Occasionally I was privy to some humorous stories. Here's one. A student sent an e-mail to his parents after his midterm exams at college. He wrote:

Dear Mom and Dad:

I'm sorry to be so long in e-mailing you lately, but my computer went down when we had a fire in my residence hall. I was overcome by smoke and rushed to the hospital. The doctor says my eyesight should be back to normal sooner or later. That wonderful resident assistant Beth, who rescued us from the fire, kindly offered to share her apartment with me until the room is cleaned up. We are going to get married. In fact, Mom and Dad, you always wanted to have grandchildren, so you should be happy to know that you will be grandparents in six months.

Please disregard the above. There was no fire, I wasn't hurt, I'm not getting married.

But ... I got a D in chemistry and an F in biology. And I want to be sure you receive this news in the proper perspective.

Your son, Jason

That creative e-mail invites us to see things in perspective. And that's what Lent is all about—getting our priorities straight. First things first. Our first priority is our relationship or life with God, and second, our life of generous service to one another, especially our families, relatives, colleagues, and friends.

The word of God carries us back over three thousand years, to a defining moment in the life of the Hebrews: their Exodus or liberation from their oppressors in ancient Egypt. Here Moses experiences the awesome presence of God in the image of "fire flaming out of a bush" (Ex 3:2).

God reveals himself as the creator of this universe: "I am the one who causes to be all that comes into existence," as one biblical author translated this mysterious phrase. And then God empowers the reluctant Moses to free the Hebrews from their oppressors. God also calls you and me, by virtue of the life-giving waters of baptism, to live a life worthy of our calling as adopted sons and daughters of God our Father, to seek always to do the right thing even when we, like Moses, are reluctant.

Paul, in his letter to the Christian community in Corinth, compares the Hebrew Exodus experience to our baptismal experience; just as God was a rock in the wilderness, out of which flowed life-giving waters, so too Christ is our rock, from whom comes our salvation, eternal life. But Paul warns us: just as the Hebrews fell from grace, so too we can fall from grace if we're not vigilant, always prepared to meet Jesus Christ in the mystery of our own death (1 Cor 10:1–6, 10-12).

Paul invites us to imagine this: if today were our last day, what would we do differently? The point is simple: don't put off to tomorrow what you can do today.

In the Gospel according to Luke, Jesus deals with the question of evil: why do bad things happen to good people? There is of course no satisfactory answer. Why so many mindless killings in Syria, why so many refugees fleeing random violence? Why the denial of basic human rights in so many places? Evil is ultimately a mystery. And then Jesus speaks about a fig tree (Lk 13:1–9).

The point of the parable is this: yes, God is patient, but one day God will hold us accountable for our lives, our attitudes, and our behaviors. And so Jesus urges us to repent *now*, to turn to a God-centered/

other-centered life. Know who you are, fragile creatures in the presence of an awesome creator, and know your destiny, life or relationship with God here and beyond this earthly life. And so let us always be vigilant. For the end, our death, could come unexpectedly.

Lent is a time to ask ourselves, who are we? What are we living for? What is our purpose in life? And how to integrate these questions into the here and now.

So often, people live in the future, not in the present. Some imagine, *My life will begin when I get a new job, when I get my degree, when I rebuild my home, when my son or daughter gets well, when my retirement is fully funded.* Life will begin in the future?

Naomi Levy, in her book *Hope Will Find You*, wrote that while caring for her critically ill daughter, she wondered when could she realize the dreams and goals she had for herself. She wrote: "I could see the ways I had been promising myself there was a future waiting for me. And just then something snapped inside my soul: This *is* my future: the present, the here and now. I'd been walking around thinking, this isn't my life; my life is coming; it's just around the bend." She thought of all the people she knew who were chanting that same line. She realized, "We were all caught in the same lie. We were fooling ourselves into thinking our lives hadn't begun. But all of us have to learn to live inside the imperfect lives we have here and now."

Today, Jesus urges us to repent, to live our everyday lives to the fullest, to live each day as though it's our last day. This Lenten season is a time for finding our way out of our winters of negativity, our deserts of self-absorption, our wildernesses of disappointments, images that weave in and out of Lent.

These days before Easter are a time for deciding what we believe to be truly important and meaningful, and then acting on our beliefs today. For the only thing we can count on is today. We can't do anything about yesterday, and we don't know about tomorrow.

Our Christian faith proclaims that life has meaning, that there is indeed an all-good, compassionate, and merciful God who seeks us out in our everyday experiences. This God became incarnate in Jesus of Nazareth. He renewed God's covenant with us and opened up to us life beyond this earthly life. God is alive among us today by the power of the Spirit, especially in the sacramental life of our global Catholic community. This is the mystery of the triune God, a God who is one yet diverse, stable yet dynamic, transcendent yet immanent!

And we can participate in God's triune life not only here and now but hereafter by living a life of regular prayer, by fasting from attitudes and behaviors that jeopardize our relationship with God and with one another, and by living a life of generous service to one another.

That is our Lenten message. I think this quote, attributed to Stephen Grellet, sums it up:

> I shall pass through this world but once:
> any good therefore that I can do
> or any kindness that I can show to any human being,
> let me do it now, let me not defer or neglect it
> for I shall not pass this way again.
> Try not to live a life of regrets.

Fourth Sunday of Lent

This Sunday is known as Laetare Sunday. Laetare is a Latin word meaning "rejoice."

Why rejoice? We are close to celebrating the Easter mystery.

I just read about a flight from Boston to Dublin, Ireland. Shortly after takeoff, the lead flight attendant announced, "Ladies and gentlemen, I'm so sorry, but it appears that there has been a terrible mix-up in our catering service. I don't know how this happened, but we have one hundred passengers, and we received only fifty dinner meals. I truly apologize." She continued, "Anyone who is kind enough to give up his or her meal so someone else can eat will receive free unlimited drinks for the five-hour flight." Two hours later, the attendant announced, "We still have those fifty dinners available." So much for priorities. But after all, Guinness beer began as an alternative to bad water. So says an interesting book, *The Search for God and Guinness*.

Now what does the word of God have to say to us today?

In the Gospel, we have the parable of the prodigal son, or better, the parable of the forgiving father. The parable has many levels of meaning. The younger son asked for his inheritance, got it, and then squandered it—and then "he comes to his senses." An incredible phrase! He realizes his true identity as a beloved son of his father. He wants to be in relationship with his father, who unconditionally forgives and loves him and gives him a welcome-home party. But the older son finds this unconditional forgiveness and love and lavish generosity incomprehensible. And rightly so, from a human point of view. But from a divine point of view, the story emphasizes God the Father's unconditional love for us. God's love for us is as crazy as the love of the father for the younger son (Lk 15:1–3, 11–32).

This may prompt us to think about disputes among siblings. Or it may move us to ponder forgiving someone who has wronged us. Some people become so fixated that they let these wrongs imprison them, so to speak. This parable challenges us to forgive. If we can't forgive on our own, pray for the grace to participate in the forgiveness of Jesus, who pardons those who are truly sorry and try to start their lives afresh.

We often read or know about people wronged by someone. This parable invites us to see ourselves in the characters. Are we the forgiving parent? The repentant younger son? The resentful older son?

The author of the book of Joshua describes how the Hebrews had crossed the Jordan River into the promised land from their wanderings in the wilderness, and how they celebrated the Passover in which they renewed God's covenant with them. God would care for his people with rich, fertile land (Jos 5:9, 10-12). This challenges us to deepen our covenantal relationships with God and one another.

Paul, in this letter to the Christian community at Corinth in Greece, says we are new creatures, alive with the life of the triune God. This triune God—Father, Son, and Spirit—within us makes us ambassadors for Jesus Christ, healers and peacemakers, generous with our time and talent, especially in our families and with our colleagues and our neighbors in the community (2 Cor 5:17–21).

Paul made Jesus the center of his life, and so should we. But who is this Jesus? Did you ever wonder what Jesus really looked like? You probably heard about the Shroud of Turin in Italy. Whether or not it's authentic, there's a solid tradition from at least the Middle Ages that says that the shroud has the imprint of the crucified Jesus. That's one portrait or face of Jesus. The great painters also give us different portraits of Jesus: da Vinci; Raphael; Michelangelo; El Greco; Rembrandt. Do you have your own favorite portrait of Jesus?

And did you know that the four recognized Gospel writers, Mark, Matthew, Luke, and John, also give us four different portraits or faces of Jesus, and also different ways in which to follow Jesus? That's easy to understand. People who know us well see us differently too, don't they?

The Gospels are not biographies; rather, they're testimonies about who Jesus is.

The Gospel writers faced a unique challenge. How portray someone who is completely human and yet completely divine? Should they overemphasize the divine or the human?

Moreover, they wrote to different audiences, so they wrote differently. We do the same. We write differently to different people. Which Gospel is most authentic? Which best reflects the historical Jesus? They all do.

Let me suggest we read one or two Gospels during the closing days of this Lenten season, perhaps Mark or John. Mark was the earliest of the writers, and the briefest. He wrote between AD 65–70, shortly after scores of Christians perished in Rome during the persecution of Emperor Nero. Many Christians were asking, "Where is God in the midst of our sufferings? Has God forgotten us?" And possibly because so many disciples were being martyred, Mark thought he ought to write who Jesus was, what he did, and what he taught. Tradition has it that Mark was a companion of Peter, a good source of information about Jesus.

Mark is an action Gospel. No mention of the birth or childhood of Jesus. He begins his drama right away with John the Baptizer in the wilderness. The Jesus in Mark seems very approachable, very human. We can easily relate to the feelings of Jesus: compassionate with the handicapped; tough with hypocrites; misunderstood by the disciples; angry with the buyers and traders in the temple; afraid in the Garden of Gethsemane; abandoned on the cross. Yes, the Jesus in Mark is very human, the Messiah who suffers so that we can live forever. And what happened to Jesus, Mark says, can happen to us too. To be a disciple may mean enduring chronic illness, making sacrifices, feeling underappreciated, giving generously to other people (e.g., our families, relatives, friends).

Luke and Matthew are similar to Mark. That's why we call these three synoptic Gospels.

The Gospel of John is a different Gospel. Jesus in John is noble, majestic, and divine. Remember how this Gospel opens: in the beginning was the Word. Yes, Jesus is completely human and completely divine. This is the mystery of the Incarnation. Jesus is one with the God of Israel. In fact, he is God. Jesus in John is the revealer of the mystery of

God, the face of God among us. To be a disciple, for John, is to have friendship or relationship with Jesus, especially in regular prayer.

Can we have different portraits or faces of Jesus? Yes, of course. Jesus, the God-man, is more than any one person can adequately describe in human language. Each Gospel writer chose to bring out certain attributes or characteristics of Jesus. The Gospels give us different faces of Jesus, different pathways in which to follow Jesus, especially during this Lenten season. And so the question we might ask now is this: how do we reflect Jesus in our daily attitudes and behaviors? Rediscover a portrait of Jesus by prayerfully reading the Gospel according to Mark or John. And let that portrait fire you up to become an ever-more-faithful disciple of Jesus, the master.

FIFTH SUNDAY OF LENT

You may have heard about the fire-and-brimstone preacher who thundered from the pulpit, "Everyone in this parish is going to die."

An elderly man in the first pew burst out laughing.

Annoyed, the preacher thundered even louder, "I said, everyone in this parish is going to die." Again, the man laughed. The preacher shouted, "What's so funny?" The man answered, "I don't belong to this parish." Someday he'll have the surprise of his life.

Seriously, the word of God for the fifth Sunday of Lent has two powerful Gospel readings from John: one if we're celebrating the "examination" for the candidates who will receive the sacraments of Initiation at the Easter Vigil; and the second Gospel for the other liturgies.

In John, chapter 11, just proclaimed to us, we have the Lazarus story. A good friend of Jesus becomes ill; his sisters send word to Jesus, "He whom you love is ill."

And what does Jesus do? Rush off to Bethany and heal his friend? No, Jesus delays for two days. And when he finally goes, his friend has been in the tomb for four days.

Lazarus's sister Martha is more than a little upset, saying, "If you had been here, my brother would not have died." Jesus responds. "I am the resurrection and the life ... they who believe in me will live ..." And then Jesus calls Lazarus back to physical life. Jesus cries out, "Lazarus, come out!" And out comes Lazarus, hands and feet bound with burial wrappings and his face covered with a burial cloth. Jesus said, "Untie him and let him go."

Two things always puzzled me about this passage. If Jesus really loved Lazarus, why didn't he rush immediately to Lazarus when he heard he was ill? Instead, Jesus stayed where he was for another two days. Second, "Jesus wept." They probably were tears of friendship. A friend was gone. And Jesus didn't have a chance to say goodbye. But then Jesus gave Lazarus a second chance, so to speak. He brought Lazarus back to physical life.

I wonder whether this second chance changed Lazarus's life dramatically. Did he do anything differently? In some ways, we are like Lazarus. We have been given so many second chances. But are we doing anything differently in light of these second chances?

The point of the Lazarus story is that Jesus is our resurrection and life. Jesus conquered death by his own dying/rising. Jesus dies/rises to inaugurate our resurrection.

We are new creatures, adopted sons and daughters of God our Father, called to live a God-centered life, a life worthy of our calling. Yes, God is alive in us, and we are alive in God. We leave behind the burial wrappings of vice, so to speak, so that we can put on virtue. We are in relationship with God and destined to be in relationship with God. That is our ultimate destiny.

Lazarus symbolizes the faithful disciple of Jesus, the true believer who will live.

In the Gospel of John for the other liturgies this weekend, from chapter 8, Jesus meets the woman caught in an adulterous relationship. I wonder if the nineteenth-century author Nathaniel Hawthorne read this story before he wrote *The Scarlet Letter*. It is all about sin, guilt, and the letter A for adulterer. Resentment, revenge, and violence in Puritan New England. How many had to read that book in school?

And did you know that Rose Hawthorne, the founder of the Hawthorne Dominican Sisters, was Nathaniel's daughter? These sisters today care for terminally ill cancer patients.

Anyway, did you ever wonder what Jesus wrote on the ground that day? Was he doodling? Was it a gesture of silence? Was he asking God for advice? And what about the man who was as guilty as the woman?

In so many words, Jesus says to us in this story, "Don't be so negatively judgmental about other people." All of us need forgiveness. That's why Jesus came: to forgive, heal, transform us, to save us from death and propel us into a glorious future, like Jesus did to this down-and-out woman.

This story invites you and me to reflect on our own willingness to forgive people who have wronged us, intentionally or unintentionally. Jesus says forgiveness is a primary characteristic of discipleship.

There's a folk wisdom that says "forgive and forget." But sometimes we can't forgive unless we remember—for example, a once-happy relationship. Then a wrong done. Finally, a shattered relationship. Perhaps we may have contributed to that. We have to forgive ourselves as well as others so that we can move forward with our lives.

Let me illustrate with a favorite book, *The Hiding Place*, in which Corrie Ten Boom describes how she lectured throughout post-WWII Europe about the need to forgive one another. Some of you already know the story. Following one of her talks, a former SS guard came up to her. He didn't recognize her, but she recognized him immediately. And suddenly, she remembered the laughing guards, the heaps of clothes on the floor, the frightened face of her own sister. And when this repentant former SS guard extended his hand to shake hers, she, who had preached so often about forgiveness, kept her hand at her side as she began to have angry, raging, and vengeful thoughts about this man.

And then she remembered: Jesus Christ had died for this man and forgives him. "Lord Jesus," she prayed, "forgive me and help me to forgive him."

She tried to smile, to raise her hand. But she couldn't. And so again she breathed a silent prayer: "Jesus, I can't forgive him for what he did to my sister and so many other people. Give me your forgiveness."

She discovered that forgiveness depended not upon her but upon God's grace. When Jesus tells us to love our enemies, he also gives us the grace to love, to forgive.

To forgive as Christ forgives is sometimes impossible to do on our own. It calls for a humility, a generosity, a spirit of compassion that is beyond most people. But Christ doesn't ask us to forgive on our own. He simply asks that we participate in his gift of forgiveness.

Forgiveness is an act of the will that overrides feeling about someone who has wronged us.

God has already forgiven—and all he asks us to do is to participate. Forgiveness is possible, not when we try to forgive on our own but when we trust in God to bring healing and forgiveness and reconciliation to our broken relationships. And as God constantly searches out the lost and the stranger, so should we.

My good friends, the Lazarus story invites us to remember our true destiny: not death but life, eternal life in relationship with God and one another.

And the story of the adulterous woman invites us to forgive one another as Jesus forgave.

Forgiveness can be a long journey, but at the end lies freedom and new life. Forgiveness transforms someone down and out into a person of hope.

I pray that God will give all of us the grace to participate in the forgiveness of Christ so that we can be at peace with oneself and one another and God, as true disciples of Jesus.

Palm Sunday
of the Lord's Passion

O ur global Catholic community on Ash Wednesday invited us to treat ourselves to those age-old exercises of prayer, fasting (or doing without those negative attitudes and behaviors that can jeopardize our relationship with God and one another), and almsgiving (or sharing what we have with one another) so that we can deepen our relationship with God and our fellow human beings. I hope these exercises during the Lenten season have reinvigorated us.

Today, Palm Sunday, we begin Holy Week, the chief week of the liturgical year. We focus in particular upon the Paschal Mystery (the dying and rising of Jesus), the journey of Jesus from this earthly life through the mystery of death into a transformative, transfigured heavenly life. The word "paschal" refers to the Hebrew Passover, or the passing of the angel of death over the homes of the Hebrews in ancient Egypt (a passing over that spared their firstborn child from death).

In a larger sense, Passover refers to the Exodus or liberation of the Hebrews from their oppressors. Every year, the Jewish community reexperiences this Exodus or liberation in the so-called Seder service, which they celebrate in April.

This Palm Sunday, we reflect upon a paradox of triumph and tragedy: the triumphal entry of Jesus into Jerusalem on the one hand, and the Gospel proclamation of the passion and death of Jesus on the other. And even in the tragedy of Good Friday, there is the triumph of Easter—Jesus, crucified, risen, and alive among us.

The word of God from Isaiah, chapter 50, is a poem about a "servant" who suffers for us (the early Christian community saw Jesus in this servant).

Paul's letter to the Christian community at Philippi quotes an early Christian hymn about God who became one of us, obedient even to death on the cross. And because of this, God greatly exalted him (Phil 2:6–11).

And the Gospel according to Luke, chapters 22–23, proclaims the passion and death of Jesus.

Next Thursday, Friday, and Saturday are known as the triduum (from a Latin word meaning a period of three days).

On Thursday, we commemorate the Lord's Supper: there is the washing of feet (a symbol of service) and then the eating of a meal—a sacrificial meal—in which Jesus gives himself to us in the signs of bread and wine (a symbol of our oneness not only with God but also our oneness with our fellow human beings).

On Good Friday, we meditate upon the passion and death of Jesus: the Garden of Gethsemane; the trial; the Crucifixion; the burial; the veneration of the cross; and then a simple Communion service.

And at the Easter vigil, we will reflect upon the passage of Jesus from this earthly life through death into a transformative, transfigured heavenly life. The resurrection is a pledge of our own liberation from death or nothingness into eternal life. The vigil includes fire (a symbol of Jesus as the light who illuminates the darkness around us); the proclamation of the story of our salvation in the scriptures; the baptism of our candidates; renewal of our own baptismal promises; and the Eucharist.

Easter proclaims that Jesus is risen, alive among us, and especially alive in the sacramental life of our global Catholic community.

This is indeed the paramount week of our liturgical year, and I urge all to participate in these services as much as you can.

Let me conclude with a favorite story of mine about a ship, the *Deutschland*, that ran aground off the coast of England in 1875. Unlike the *Titanic*, the *Deutschland* had enough lifeboats and life preservers. But it did no good. Fierce gale winds swamped the boats. The passengers were told to go to the deck. There, they could see the lights of the shore. But no one saw the ship's distress signals.

Among the 157 passengers who perished were five Franciscan nuns traveling to Missouri for a new teaching ministry. They were immortalized in a poem to which I will allude in a moment.

According to reports, these five nuns, fleeing Otto von Bismarck's anti-Catholic legislation in 1873, stayed below deck because there wasn't enough room on deck. And as the poem reads:

As the water rose around them, the nuns clasped hands and were heard saying,
"O Christus, O Christus, komm schnell" or "O Christ, O Christ, come quickly!"

The English Jesuit Gerard Manley Hopkins was profoundly moved by the newspaper accounts of this tragedy and wrote a poem about it, *The Wreck of the Deutschland*, which he dedicated to these five nuns. He saw in their deaths a parallel to the sufferings of Jesus for the sake of the many.

Hopkins concludes the poem with this line referring to Christ: "Let him easter in us, be a dayspring to the dimness of us …"

As used in this poem, the word "easter" is a nautical term. It means steering a craft toward the east, into the light. And that light is Jesus Christ. Yes, "Let Christ easter in us" so that we may reflect his life by practicing virtue—for example, compassion, peacemaking, fairness, truth, and forgiveness. "Let Christ easter in us" so that he may empower us to be healers, teachers, and foot washers like him. "Let Christ easter in us" so that he may give us courage to bear our crosses as he bore his cross for us.

Yes, throughout these forty days of Lent, we have been striving to steer our lives toward the light of Jesus Christ, trying to shake off the darkness around us and the burdens of our daily lives.

I pray that this Holy Week will inspire us to seek ever more enthusiastically the God who became flesh in Jesus of Nazareth and who by his death and resurrection opened up to all humankind a transformative, transfigured life beyond earthly life; a God who is alive among us by the power of the Spirit.

And then in the moment of our own dying, we, like those five Franciscan nuns in the poem, will be able to pray, "O Christ, O Christ, come quickly so that you can easter or live in us, as our light forever."

Holy Thursday, Evening Mass of the Lord's Supper

We begin the Easter Triduum with the Mass of the Lord's Supper. We remember the institution of the Eucharist, the institution of the ministerial priesthood, and love for one another in the symbolic washing of the feet.

I would like to reflect on ministerial priesthood—what it was, what it is, and the essential continuity.

I was ordained in Washington, DC, in the middle of the 1960s, a decade of incredible change in our country and in our church. There was the civil rights movement, the assassinations of two Kennedys and Martin Luther King Jr. among others, the Vietnam War protests, city and campus riots, the Soviet invasion of Czechoslovakia, and the Second Vatican Council.

Our everyday life as priests-in-training had a rhythm of prayer and study. There was daily Mass (with less emphasis on the Liturgy of the Word), the Liturgy of the Hours, friendly visits to the Blessed Sacrament chapel, and the recitation of the Rosary.

And the classroom lectures? The approach to graduate theological studies was generally apologetic; in other words, "shooting at where the enemy was last seen, whoever that was," as a classmate described the pedagogy. Imaginary "straw men" were set up to be "slain."

This approach was quite different from today's. The church today is incredibly different from the church of the sixties. Yet, despite differences, there is a continuity.

Many of us read *The Diary of a Country Priest* by Georges Bernanos. One freely translated line summed up what ministerial priesthood is all about: it is grace that matters, and grace permeates everything. That's what priesthood is all about, a life that gives grace by being grace. Yes, the priest is to be an instrument of grace to others, one who proclaims that all is grace because, like the Master he serves, he has come to give full life to the people he serves.

Ministerial priesthood is a sacrament, a symbolic or ritual act of incorporation into the sphere of Christ's mission. The bishop, through the laying on of hands and the consecratory prayer, confers upon the ordinand a unique relationship, enabling him to function "in persona Christi": preaching, celebrating the sacraments, pastoring people. This relationship is essentially different from the relationship to Jesus in baptism.

The priest, in light of the New Testament, is a disciple of Jesus, chosen by God to be an apostle, set apart to proclaim the person and mission of Jesus in the community. He is a presbyter, responsible for its pastoral care, and a presider at the Eucharist where he gathers together the community, celebrates the presence of the living Christ, and sends the community forth to witness the living Christ.

The capacity for leadership in a faith community, I believe, is key to the identity of the priest. Here I would enumerate some effective priestly characteristics: an awareness of God's presence in one's life and in the lives of others; empathy; the ability to relate and enable; courage; loyalty to Catholic traditions; hope; a sense of mission; and an ability to verbalize the content of faith.

The Second Vatican Council decree *Presbyterorum Ordinis* (*On the Ministry and Life of Priests*) reflects a biblical understanding of priestly ministry. The priest participates in Christ's priesthood and in his mediation between God and men and women. In other words, the priest proclaims the good news, shepherds the faithful, and celebrates the sacred mysteries. The priest is one chosen and empowered by God to continue the mission of Jesus Christ as Prophet, Priest, and King and, thereby, lead all others in the household of faith to that fullness of mission appropriate to their baptismal call.

The priest is indeed God's servant to God's people. Jesus Christ, in effect, says to the priest, "Take my hands as yours with which to bless and to sanctify and to consecrate; take my eyes and see my image in every person with whom you come into contact; take my arms and let them embrace those who are lonely and lost; take my feet and let them lead you to sinners and reclaim them for me. For I see and I hear and I think and I feel and I love in you. For you no longer live, but Christ lives in you."

I conclude with some truths that the eminent American Catholic historian Rev. John Tracy Ellis gave to candidates for the priesthood at a commencement I presided over many years ago:

- "Hold tenaciously to the enduring principle that there is a right and a wrong in human affairs, regardless of how much a hedonistic society seeks to eradicate that truth from your lives."
- "Resist with all the force you can summon the pervasive tendency to succumb to the herd instinct and to follow the majority wherever it may lead, recalling the salutary axiom of

Archbishop John Ireland of St. Paul-Minneapolis, 'The timid move in crowds, the brave in single file.' Thus you will resist one of the most menacing aspects influencing human conduct in our time."

- "Learn to live with mystery, and to accept with serenity the truth embodied in the oft-quoted remark of Adrian van Kaam to the effect that 'Life is a mystery to be lived, not a problem to be solved.'"

- "Trust the Church to answer more questions than any other institution about life's baffling problems, but do not expect her to answer them all, for there are questions to which there is no answer this side of eternity."

- "Finally, at intervals give thoughtful consideration to the end of life, knowing you cannot foretell its time or circumstance, yet fully reconciled to its inevitability, and in that regard make your own the prayer of that noble layman, Saint Thomas More, when he said: 'Good Lord, give me the grace so to spend my life, that when the day of my death shall come, though I feel pain in my body, I may feel comfort in soul, and with faithful hope of thy mercy, in due love towards thee and charity towards the world, I may, through thy grace, part hence into thy glory.'"

Yes, Jesus Christ in his death and in his resurrection became the source of divine life. May Christ gift priests in their ministry with that source of life so that they may be sources of life, wellsprings capable of bestowing the water of life upon those they serve.

GOOD FRIDAY
OF THE LORD'S PASSION

For Good Friday, I began to think of the last words ascribed to Jesus on the cross at Calvary. Sin of course is the backdrop of the cross. God became one of us in Jesus so that we could become one with God. Sin severed us from God, broke a relationship. Sin also severed us within ourselves; we were made in God's image, and then we clouded the image of God.

The Gospel according to John summed up the solution in the third chapter: "God so loved the world that he gave his only Son, so that everyone who believes in him might not perish but might have eternal life" (Jn 3:16).

Jesus experienced what Godforsaken-ness feels like and died as we die but with faith in his Father, with hope of life eternal. I invite you to meditate upon the last words ascribed to Jesus and ask how they can be a guide in our own lives.

"Father, forgive them."

One word can sum up Jesus's life: compassion. He is compassion incarnate. Calvary is the climax of his compassion. Jesus cries out, "Father, forgive them." Forgiveness and reconciliation are what Good Friday is all about. Yes, we can be one with God, share the life of Father, Son, and Spirit alive within us. With God's grace, we can be at peace within ourselves and with the power of the Spirit love our brothers and sisters as Christ loves me and them. And so we pray in the Lord's prayer, "Forgive us our debts as we forgive our debtors" (Mt 6:12).

To the extent that I forgive others, to that extent, dear Lord, I want you to forgive me. And if we cannot forgive on our own, we pray for the grace to participate in Jesus's forgiveness of us.

"Today you will be with me in Paradise."

Three men are crucified together. Two probably were robbers. One robber shouts to the man in the middle, "Are you not the Messiah? Save yourself and us" (Lk 23:39). The other robber surprisingly acknowledges Jesus's kingly status: "Jesus, remember me when you come into your kingdom." Jesus's reply to that is equally surprising: "Today you will be with me in Paradise."

Here is the story of salvation. One robber admits he's a sinner and is sorry for his sins; he asks this stranger, this just man, this "king" to remember him. And Jesus responds, "Today you will be with me." The other robber wants all three to come down from their crosses. Yes, the cross is our way to salvation. Jesus refuses to come down from the cross because God so loved us. The good thief discovered salvation not by coming down from the cross but by being crucified with Jesus.

May we carry our daily inescapable crosses out of love for Jesus so that we may hear the words the good thief heard: "you will be with me."

"Woman, behold your son ... Behold your mother."

Here is a mother who first lost her husband and now is losing her only son. "Look!" Jesus murmurs to his mother. Then to John: "Look!" And from that hour, the disciple took her into his home (Jn 19:26–27).

In the climactic moment of our salvation, we are recreated as sons and daughters of God our Father. John stands for all Christians; Mary represents the church, which brings forth sons and daughters modeled after Jesus. Mary with John symbolize the relationship that must bind sons and daughters to their mother. Mary is the mother of God's only begotten Son. She's the disciple par excellence. Beneath the cross, Mary stands for the church that brought me to new life in baptism, enlightens my mind with God's word, feeds my soul at the Lord's Supper, and holds me dying like the mother in Michelangelo's *Pieta*.

Yes, the church is holy yet full of sinners. It challenges us to focus on the things of God yet seems preoccupied with the things of earth. Yet in this church I find my strength, my support, and my joy. The church is my mother. May I always trust the church to answer the fundamental questions of human life: Who am I? What is the purpose of my life? Trust the church to answer life's baffling questions but don't expect every answer, for there are questions to which there is no answer this side of eternity.

"My God, why have you forsaken me?"

At about 3 p.m. on a dark Friday, a crucified Jesus cried out, "My God, my God, why have you forsaken me?" (Mt 27:46). How can this be? The God who said, "This is my beloved Son, with whom I am well pleased" (Mt 3:17) now is absent. How can this be? Perhaps Jesus was simply reciting Psalm 22. No. Jesus felt loneliness, abandonment, Godforsaken-ness. But he never stopped trusting.

Loneliness seems to go hand in hand with life. God strips away our attachments: people we love, things we cherish, life itself. But God doesn't forsake us unless we forsake God. No matter what, God is there. Think of Isaiah 49: "Can a mother forget her infant ... Even should she forget, I will never forget you." The point is this: may we always sense the presence of God in the challenges of life, especially in the liturgy and in people who may cry, "God, why have you forsaken me?"

"I thirst."

Jesus was physically thirsty. How could he not be? But the question remains: was physical thirst uppermost in Jesus's mind? Remember Jesus kneeling in the Garden of Gethsemane: "My Father, if it is possible, let this cup pass from me; yet, not as I will, but as you will." Jesus thirsted to drink the cup of suffering and dying. Why? Because only then would his Father's will be fulfilled. Jesus wanted to complete what he had been born to do. More than anything else in life, he wanted to die. For us. Out of love. The cup is our suffering, our dying.

Saint Paul put it well when he wrote: "Now I rejoice in my sufferings for your sake, and in my flesh I am filling up what is lacking in the afflictions of Christ on behalf of his body, which is the Church" (Col 1:24).

Mother Teresa, for example, sought to satisfy her thirst by touching the image of God hidden especially in the poor.

May my daily prayer be: dear Lord, I am thirsty; please awaken your Spirit within me, to inflame my heart, so that you may satisfy my thirst by letting me touch the image of God hidden in so many people around me.

"It is finished."

Jesus hangs helplessly from the cross and quietly utters, "It is finished" (Jn 19:30).

What is finished? His mission from his heavenly Father is now completed. Incredible love is consummated in horrific crucifixion. God could have redeemed us otherwise. So why crucifixion? It's a mystery. The First Letter of Peter gives a hint: "Christ also suffered for you, leaving you an example that you should follow in his footsteps" (1 Pet 2:21). And God clearly felt we could learn how to love if we saw how Jesus loved. "The way we came to know love was that he laid down his life for us; so we ought to lay down our lives for our brothers" (1 Jn 3:16). Jesus's work is not finished until God's favor, God's love touches all humankind. When we touch men and women with God's favor and God's love, then we are finishing the work Jesus came to do. And then in our own final Calvary, we can murmur with Christ to the Father, "The work you gave me to do—it is finished."

May God inspire us to be instruments of God's favor and love to the people around us.

"Into your hands I commend my Spirit."

These words can be found in Psalm 31. Jesus surrendered himself in his death unconditionally to the absolute mystery that he called his

Father, into whose hands he committed his existence when in his dying everything seemed to fall away from him. Death was the most radical act of faith. Jesus died with faith in his Father, with trust in God's love, with hope that he would live forever.

Death, for Jesus, was a descent into darkness. It was with such faith, such hope, such trust that he could cry out with a loud voice, "Father, into your hands I commend my spirit" (Lk 23:46).

God asks of us that we too, once and for all, let go of our earthbound existence, all we call human living: home, loved ones, possessions, my very self. It's a movement into darkness. But for the Christian, life is Christ, and death is gain. When Jesus cried, "Into your hands I commend my Spirit," he was affirming life. Beyond death is life.

May God give me the grace to utter these words with faith in God's love and with the hope of life with God forever. May these seven words ascribed to Jesus inspire us to live our lives in such a manner that in the moment of our dying, we will have faith in God's unconditional love for us and hope in life eternal.

EASTER OF THE RESURRECTION OF THE LORD

Happy Easter! Felices Pascuas! Joyeuses Paques! Buona Pasqua! Frohe Ostern!

I remember a young couple invited me to their home for a festive dinner years ago. I asked their little boy what we were having. He said, "Goat."

I said, "Goat? Are you sure?"

"Yep," he said. "Daddy said to Mommy, 'Today is as good as any to have the old goat for dinner." We had chicken Cordon Bleu.

The word "Easter" comes from "Eastre," the name of a Saxon goddess of the dawn or spring. Easter symbolizes life. Jesus is alive!

Easter brings back childhood memories. We used to color eggs with designs or go egg hunting. The Easter egg can symbolize the struggle of the chick to free itself from its shell to take flight into a much bigger world beyond itself. But for this to happen, the egg has to go to pieces. New life demands shattering the old.

We too as disciples of Jesus struggle to break through a world that we may perceive is going to pieces so that we can take flight into God's eternal dwelling place. More precisely, we believe that in the mystery of our own dying, we will break out of our own earthly shell, so to speak, so that we can experience a new transformative, transfigured heavenly life.

Easter is about the dawn, daybreak, starting over, beginning again. Jesus's resurrection is a new day for all of us. Every morning, we wake up and we have another chance to start over. Perhaps when we went to bed the night before, we still carried the burdens of the day just ending: things undone or put off, bad things said, good things unsaid. In the morning all is possibility, all is opportunity. We begin again.

Who among us is content with who we are? Who is content with things as they are? Who among us does not want to be more loving, more generous, more tenderhearted, more thoughtful, more helpful? Who wouldn't want the courage to act upon our convictions as opposed to our fears? Who among us doesn't know a heart to heal, a broken relationship to mend, a lost soul to find?

This Easter, God wakes us up again. It is a new day. Let this be the morning to start again, to repair the broken, to rediscover God's extraordinary grace transforming our ordinary lives.

In the word of God today, Peter proclaims the kerygma, the proclamation of the good news. Peter speaks about all that God has done for us through Jesus of Nazareth. Jesus was baptized by John, anointed with the Spirit, and went about the countryside of Judea and Galilee working signs and wonders, proclaiming that the kingdom of God was beginning to break into our lives. Eventually Jesus was crucified but then burst forth out of the tomb and was lifted up to his heavenly Father so that He could draw all of us to himself into a new heavenly life (Acts 10:34–43).

Yes, Jesus is alive, and because He lives, we also live. He is indeed, Peter shouts, a God of mercy and forgiveness. And that's why Pope Francis emphasizes that the church is a field hospital, here to heal wounds.

Paul, in his letter to the Christian community in Colossae, Turkey, challenges us to seek God in our everyday lives so that we might appear with him in glory at the end-time.

And in the Gospel according to John, chapter 20, we hear the story of the resurrection of Jesus.

Mary Magdalene comes to the tomb only to find it empty; she summons Peter and John who go in. The disciples discovered that Jesus is not among the dead. He is risen. He is alive. He has passed from earthly life through the mystery of death into a new, transfigured heavenly reality. And this heavenly reality is ours as well. That is the Easter message!

Some of you may have seen the Vietnam Memorial in Washington, DC. The arms of the long, V-shaped, polished black granite wall point toward the Washington Monument and the Lincoln Memorial. And on the wall are inscribed the 58,000 plus names of men and women killed or missing in the Vietnam War. From time to time, I would find and read a letter at the foot of that wall that a son or daughter wrote home, perhaps their last. I've often thought, *How many hopes lie buried here*. These soldiers were full of life, with so many dreams. And suddenly they were dead.

And then I thought about Easter. The disciples of Jesus, huddled in the upper room in Jerusalem, could have said the same thing: "How many hopes lie buried here." The disciples who met Jesus on the road to Emmaus could have said the same. And yet, forty-some hours after those hopes were buried, the risen Christ appeared to Mary Magdalene outside the tomb, to the disciples in the upper room, and to the two disciples on the road to Emmaus. Jesus was not simply a spirit or ghost; nor was he simply resuscitated. Otherwise, they would have recognized him immediately.

Yes, it was a bodily resurrection; the earthly and crucified Jesus was the same person as the resurrected Jesus. But he was transfigured or transformed into a new reality. Jesus said to the disciples, "I live, and because I live, we also live."

How? No sooner are we born in the flesh than we are reborn in the Spirit. Water is poured upon us in the rite of baptism, and in these waters the Spirit of God is poured out upon us, and a new life is ours. The triune God lives within us, and we live within the triune God. As we grow into adolescence, the bishop anoints our forehead with oil in the sign of the cross—and in that gesture, God confirms and pours out more fully the gifts of the Spirit so that we might practice more faithfully the fruits of the Spirit.

And at this Eucharist, where the living Christ sacramentally presences himself to us in the signs of bread and wine, where he mystically reenacts his redemptive, salvific activity and becomes one with us ever so briefly in Communion, the living Christ feeds us with his life so we can continue our journey. And if we should stumble on our journey, the living Christ lifts us up in the rite of penance where we celebrate God's mercy.

Yes, through the sacraments, privileged encounters with God, we experience the living Christ. In the exchange of wedding promises, God strengthens the love between husband and wife. In anointing of the sick, God heals our wounds. All the sacraments are indeed signs of God's care for us as we journey to our heavenly dwelling place.

Eternal life in relationship with God and one another—that is our ultimate purpose. In the mystery of our own dying, we believe we will make an evolutionary leap into a new reality, as Jesus already has. Ours is indeed a faith in a new day, a fresh start again. Easter is about getting our priorities straight. First things first. Easter is about asking, "How can we be more loving, more generous, more tenderhearted, more thoughtful, more helpful?" Easter is about finding a heart to heal, a relationship to mend, a lost soul to find. It's a new dawn, a new day, a fresh start.

SECOND SUNDAY OF EASTER
(OR SUNDAY OF DIVINE MERCY)

You may have heard about a hooded robber who burst into a bank, ordered everyone down on the floor, and demanded that the tellers empty their cash into his bag. A brave customer pulled the robber's hood off on the way out. The robber shouted, "You saw my face!" and shot the customer. The robber then saw a teller looking straight at him. The robber shot her too. The robber then yelled, "Did anyone else see my face?" After a few moments, a longsuffering wife piped up, "My husband who's lying next to me also got a pretty good look at you." Moral: don't be at the wrong place at the wrong time.

We continue to celebrate the Easter miracle the next six Sundays: Jesus Christ lives, and because he lives, we live.

Have you ever witnessed an Easter miracle? A depressed person resurrected to hope; an alcoholic resurrected to sobriety; a troubled marriage resurrected to renewed love; an angry man resurrected to forgiveness; an estrangement between parent and child bridged; a terrible wrong forgiven.

We can create little Easter miracles for others when we seize the opportunity every day. Think about how we can create such miracles this Easter season.

Now what does the word of God have to say to us today? In the book of Acts, chapter 5, the apostles work signs and wonders, the community is growing by leaps and bounds, and a vibrant faith community is emerging. That word should inspire us to worship together as a parish community and share what we have with one another, especially our time and talents, for example in volunteer service.

The book of Revelation, which generally highlights the apocalyptic struggle between good and evil, describes a Christian by the name of John who has a visionary experience of the God-man Jesus, risen and alive, the alpha and omega, the beginning and the end, the conqueror of death. The author encourages his readers to persevere in their faith despite the hardships they're undergoing, because good ultimately will triumph (Rv 1:9–13, 17–19).

In the Gospel according to John, we have a post-resurrection appearance of Jesus in a Jerusalem house where the apostles are hiding behind locked doors. Jesus here was not simply a spirit or ghost; nor was he simply resuscitated. The earthly and crucified Jesus was the same person as the resurrected Jesus. But this earthly body of Jesus was transformed. It was, as Pope Benedict XVI phrased it, an evolutionary "leap" into a totally new reality.

In this passage, John 20:19–31, the risen Jesus bestows upon the disciples the energizing Spirit, the abiding peace, and the overwhelming mercy of God. But the skeptical Thomas wasn't there. Thomas is portrayed as the quintessential doubter. Lo and behold, a week later, Jesus appears again. And Thomas makes that awesome declaration of faith in those simple words: "My Lord and my God."

Who is this Thomas? We know little to nothing about him. The name "Thomas" is a nickname, meaning "twin" in Aramaic. But Thomas the doubter or questioner is easily identifiable with many people today. Because to be human is to question.

Christianity proposes that we were born to be in relationship with God. Otherwise, we will experience a hunger, an emptiness, a feeling that something is missing. St. Augustine, in his autobiography *Confessions*, captured this spiritual hunger eloquently: "Our hearts are restless until they can find rest in you, O God."

Leo Tolstoy, the author of *War and Peace*, wrote a book titled *A Confession*, describing his own search for meaning and purpose. He pursued it first in the carousing social circles of Moscow and Saint Petersburg, Russia. That didn't satisfy him. He then sought wealth, success, fame, status, and family. Even when Tolstoy had a loving wife and thirteen children, still one question haunted him: "Is there any meaning in my life which will not be annihilated by the inevitabilty of my death?" Eventually Tolstoy discovered that the simple farm people of Russia found the answer to these questions through their lively Christian faith—their relationship with God.

The one thing we all need is a loving, ongoing relationship. But no human relationship will satisfy us completely. There always remains something missing. That is because we were created to live in a relationship with God. Jesus said, "I am the way." He is the only One who can bring us into that relationship with God.

Sometimes I hear people say, "It doesn't matter what you believe so long as you are sincere." But it is possible to be sincerely wrong. An extreme example was Adolf Hitler, whose ideology destroyed millions of lives.

Jesus said, "I am the way, the truth, and the life." In Jesus, we find life where there was death. Yes, every human being is made in the image of God. But we are fallen human beings. It does matter what we believe. Good and bad, heroic generosity and cowardly selfishness, light and darkness, they all live within us.

The author C.S. Lewis described "our human situation" starkly when he wrote: "For the first time I examined myself. And there I found what appalled me: a zoo of lusts, a bedlam of ambitions, a nursery of fears, a harem of hatreds."

We all cry out for healing and mercy, which we celebrate today—divine mercy. We cry out for forgiveness, and only in Jesus Christ can we find it. Jesus Christ, through the mystery of his dying and rising, has freed us from death and nothingness so that we can be in relationship with God forever.

Christianity challenges us to live life authentically, to the full. It is the truth. It transforms our lives.

The twentieth-century philosopher and theologian Paul Tillich described our three fears: fear about meaninglessness; fear about death; and fear about guilt. Jesus Christ meets these fears head-on. He is the way, the truth, and the life.

One final word about Thomas the doubter, the questioner. There are all kinds of indicators pointing to God: the order in the universe presupposes an orderer (e.g., a watch presupposes a watchmaker); hope presupposes a future; moral outrage at genocide presupposes a judge; and so forth.

Of course, there are also indicators that there's no God—for example, genocide even now.

But faith in God is a calculated risk. Blaise Pascal's wager captures that. Pascal was a French mathematician, inventor, and philosopher. Pascal's wager goes like this: One does not know whether God exists. Not believing in God is bad for one's eternal soul if God indeed does exist. Believing in God is of no consequence if God does not exist. Therefore, it is in one's interest to believe in God.

Doubting Thomas concludes, "My Lord and my God." Yes, Jesus lives, and because he lives, you and I live.

Life in relationship with God forever. That is the ultimate purpose of life. Someday this earthly existence of ours, like that of Jesus crucified and risen, will be transformed, in some unimaginable way, into a heavenly existence.

At a funeral mass, we hear the words, "For those who believe, life is not taken away, life is merely changed." Let us pray that the gift of faith will empower us, like Thomas, to cry out every day, "My Lord and my God."

THIRD SUNDAY OF EASTER

Y ou may have heard about the husband who decided to surprise his
wife by painting the kitchen while she was out.

When she arrived home, she smelled fresh paint. She went into the kitchen and found her husband lying on the floor in a pool of sweat—wearing a parka and a leather jacket. She asked, "What are you doing?" He answered, "I'm trying to prove I can do something around the house."

She then wondered why he wore a parka over his leather jacket. He replied that the directions on the paint can read: For best results, put on two coats. Moral: read directions carefully.

The word of God takes us back to our first century where the apostles stand before the Jewish supreme court, so to speak, the Sanhedrin. The court wants the apostles to stop proclaiming the good news. But Peter boldly tells the court that he must obey God rather than the court.

God, Peter declares, exalted the crucified Jesus. He is alive, risen, and among us. Peter urges them to repent or refocus their lives on God and the things of God (Acts 5:27–32, 40–41).

Peter, in faith, recognized Jesus as Lord—the way, the truth, and the life—and as our Savior who invites us into a relationship with God forever. And the author also challenges us to recognize Jesus as our Lord—our way, our truth, and our life—and as our Savior who invites us into a relationship with God forever.

The book of Revelation describes a visionary, mystical, heavenly experience in which countless creatures cry out that Jesus, the Lamb slain for us, is worthy to receive power and riches, wisdom and honor, and glory and blessing (Rv 5:11–14).

The author may be asking us, do we know that through the Lamb slain, in other words the mystery of the dying and rising of Jesus, we have been blessed with the gift of a relationship with God forever?

In the Gospel according to John, chapter 21, the author highlights a post-resurrection experience of Jesus. Standing on the Galilee shore, Jesus tells the disciples, who had been fishing all night and caught nothing, to cast their nets again. Lo and behold, they make a huge catch. John recognizes the Lord. And so too does Peter, who only recently denied Jesus three times! But now the repentant Peter is ready to follow Jesus. Jesus asks Peter three times, "Do you love me enough to trust me completely? To commit yourself totally to me?" And three times Peter answers, "Yes, Lord, you know that I love you."

Jesus responds, "Feed my lambs" (i.e., "Nourish the people I entrust to you spiritually"). Jesus concludes, "When you grow old, you will become powerless." I think of Robert Browning's poem, "Grow Old along with Me." Yes, in following Jesus, even to death, Peter too will be glorified like Jesus.

Last Sunday, we met Thomas the questioner, the doubter. Today we meet Peter, the spontaneous or impulsive disciple. Who was he? Peter, aka Simon, appears to have had a good fishing business in Capernaum, on the northwest shore of the Sea of Galilee. He was uneducated but street-smart, married, left the business to become a disciple, formed his inner circle, proclaimed Jesus as the Messiah, denied him, witnessed his resurrection, became the leader or rock among the disciples, worked signs and wonders, evangelized throughout the eastern Mediterranean, and eventually was martyred in Rome. Two New Testament letters are attributed to Peter.

Although Peter often appears impetuous, he always was ready to admit a mistake, to make amends. In the end, Peter is someone you could trust, a man of character. As someone said, "The true measure of character is what you do when nobody's watching."

Within all of us, there is a tension to choose our better or our worse selves. Catholic Christianity calls this "original sin" or "the fall from grace." Something is not quite right with us.

Many try to explain why people behave the way they do. Lawrence Kohlberg, the distinguished psychologist, educator, and author, described human behavior or moral development in three "quantum leap" stages.

The first stage is self-centered, what's good for me: "I'll be good or they'll punish me," or, "I'll be good, and they will reward me." The second stage is group-centered: "I'll be loyal to the group; family, peers, and laws of society demand that I be loyal." And the final stage of development is principle or integrity centered: "I couldn't live with myself if I didn't do the right thing," or, "I will follow my principles no matter what." It's staying true to our inner best selves.

Whether you agree with that theory of moral development or not, I prefer to emphasize an informed conscience.

What is conscience? It is closely associated with our feelings—we sometimes feel guilty about things we do or don't do—yet conscience is more than feelings. Conscience is a power of judgment, our moral compass, so to speak, an almost instinctive judgment about the goodness or badness of our behavior and attitudes. Our conscience is a friendly guide in our quest for fulfillment as authentic human beings.

Leo Tolstoy, the Russian novelist, philosopher, and reformer, noted there is only one important question in life: what shall we do and how shall we live? Yes, how shall we live? Peter would answer, "By being men and women of moral character."

Now there's a difference between personality and character. Our personality on the surface puts us in a category: cheerful, or moody, or excitable, and so on. Character, by contrast, is singular and defines who we are, at the core of our inmost selves. Personality is emotional. Character is ethical. Personality is neither good nor bad. Character, by definition, is either good or bad.

Character manifests itself in the choices that each of us must make about the fundamental values or virtues by which we live. Men and women of character try to be true to their inner best selves. A person of moral character will choose the dignity of the person over impersonal business or material advantage, a respect for human beings over the lust for pleasure, power, or personal success. A person of character is willing to go the extra mile to make something "just right" because it's the better and worthy thing to do.

A person of character will speak up for what is right, defend what is fair, take a stand on principle and conscience—yes, an informed conscience. Even if it is to their disadvantage, even if others turn against them, persons of character will show courage and not simply get along by going along. They will try to choose what is true and good and right in all decisions, small and great, that affect work, career, family, relationships with others, even leisure time. They will stand for something.

And so today, the word of God invites us, among other things, to become men and women of character like Peter who, although he failed at times, still picked himself up to do what was the right thing.

Fourth Sunday of Easter

You may have heard about the preacher who died and was waiting in line at the pearly gates of heaven. Ahead of him was a fellow with sunglasses, loud shirt, leather jacket, and jeans. St. Peter asked, "Who are you?" The fellow replied, "I'm Joe, a retired pilot from Allegiant airlines." St. Peter checked his list, handed the pilot a silk robe and golden staff, and ushered him into heaven.

Next, it's the preacher's turn. "I'm Pastor Bob from Assembly of God Church." St. Peter handed him a cotton robe and a wooden staff. The surprised pastor said, "Wait! Why did he get silk and gold and I only get cotton and wood?" St. Peter replied, "We go by results here. When you preached, people dozed. When he flew, people were wide awake, praying." Airline flights sometimes can do that for you!

The word of God takes us back to St. Paul's first missionary journey through the country we know as Turkey. The spirit-filled Paul and Barnabas first spoke to the Jews about the Gospel or good news. Jesus their long-awaited Messiah, once crucified, now risen and alive, invites them into a relationship with God forever.

But some in the synagogue were outraged. So Paul and Barnabas went on to proclaim the good news to the Gentiles, the non-Jews. God gifted them with faith in Jesus Christ. They repented, focused their lives on God, and were baptized. The author may be asking, how focused are we on God? Do we try to live a God-centered life?

The book of Revelation, chapter 7, describes a vision in which a symbolic number of people are glorifying God and enjoying God's presence. Someone then asks, "Who are these people?" The answer, "They are the ones who were martyred because of their faith in Jesus Christ. They stayed true to their faith and kept their baptismal promises. They now worship God, and the Lamb leads them to life-giving waters, eternal life."

This passage (Acts 13:43–52) challenges us to stay true to our faith in Jesus Christ, especially when things are not going our way, when what is happening is the opposite of what we want to happen.

In the Gospel according to John, the author describes Jesus as our good shepherd who cares for us as we navigate the twists and turns of life on our journey toward our heavenly home (Jn 10:27–30).

Yes, Jesus Christ lives, and because he lives, we live in God's triune life. The author may be asking whether we recognize God's providence or presence or care in our own lives.

During this Easter season, we have been meeting different biblical personalities: Thomas the Questioner who professes his faith in Jesus as his Lord and his God; Peter the impetuous disciple who, no matter how many times he falls, always picks himself up and tries to do the right thing.

This week, we meet Paul, also known by his Jewish name, Saul. Born in Tarsus, southeast Turkey, he was well educated in Judaism and Greco-Roman philosophy. He was by trade a tent maker. And he also was a firebrand, a rabid persecutor of Christians.

Paul was suddenly blinded by a light from heaven as he approached Damascus in Syria. That awesome visionary experience of Jesus, crucified and now risen, turned Paul's life upside down. He became God's "chosen instrument" to the non-Jews, one of the greatest evangelizers. Often controversial but always self-confident, he lived a purpose-driven life. This religious genius established Christian faith communities throughout the eastern Mediterranean, authored letters that shaped the history of Christian thought, and eventually was beheaded by Nero.

Paul and the apostles lived and died for their faith communities. We stand on their shoulders. Without the generations of heroes and heroines before us in Catholic Christianity, we would not have our faith communities today. And our response: gratitude to God for our Catholic faith community to which we belong and which gives noble purpose to our lives.

Let me give you a few good reasons why I'm grateful:

1. We are a worldwide community of believers (one billion-plus people, men and women of all shades of language, race, and color, rich and poor, black and white, American, European, Asian, and African, charismatic and traditional), a diverse family that celebrates the presence of the risen Jesus in our liturgies and especially in our Eucharist, where the living Christ presences himself to us sacramentally in the signs of bread and wine. Yes, we have a relationship with God. The life of the triune God breathes within us, and we breathe within that life. We are the people of God, heralds of the good news, servants called to wash the feet of one another. Awesome images of the church! My favorite image is Peter's fishing boat. Why? This early Christian image symbolizes all of us. We're on a journey—together—with a map, lots of stormy weather, people slipping overboard, survivors being pulled in, mutinies, getting off course, being attacked. And a boat of course needs a captain. He may not be ideal—too lax, too strict, too single-minded (like Ahab in Herman Melville's *Moby Dick*)—but if everybody grabs the tiller, we're all in trouble. Then again, for a time, Peter wasn't ideal, yet what his crew managed to do has lasted two thousand years.

2. We are a community with splendid heroes and heroines. We know the litany of saints. These men and women lived the beatitudes. They were spiritually hungry for God; asked for forgiveness and forgave; were sincere; strove to bring peace; and expected nothing in return. They challenge us to live the beatitudes.

    Let's not practice the "devil's beatitudes." For example, blessed are the troublemakers; they shall be called my children. Blessed are the gossipers, for they are my secret agents. Blessed are the complainers; I am all ears for them. Blessed are the touchy; they may stop going to church altogether; they are my missionaries.

3. We are a community that attempts to meet the basic needs of the poor. There's an old hymn that I would like to paraphrase: Christ has no hands but our hands to do his work today. He has no feet but our feet to lead people in his way. He has no voice but our voice to tell people that he is the good news. He has no help but our help to lead folks to his side. Yes, we are the mystical body of Christ attempting to meet the needs of people, especially the poor.

    But alas we are also a community with tensions. We are human. Some people are dysfunctional and make a mess out of their lives and others. So, we have to live with some messiness and muddle through as best we can.

The word of God, especially the book of the Acts with its narrative about the missionary journeys of Paul, invites us to thank God for the heroes and heroines before us who have built up this global Catholic community. The word invites us to give thanks for the faith community to which we belong, a community that calls us to be in relationship with God forever. For that is the purpose of life—to be in relationship with God here and beyond our earthly life. Yes, be proud to belong and invite others into the spiritual riches of this community.

FIFTH SUNDAY OF EASTER

M any of us as youngsters had to memorize lines from Shakespeare's plays. Lines such as "To thine own self be true," or, "All the world's a stage, and all the men and women are merely players: and one man in his time plays many parts, his acts being seven ages," from infant to schoolboy and so forth.

Someone compared the seven ages to seven stages of prayer. At twenty, we pray we will wake up romantic. At thirty, we pray we will wake up married. At forty, we pray we will wake up successful. At fifty, we pray we will wake up rich. At sixty, we pray we will wake up contented. At seventy, we pray we will wake up healthy. And at eighty, we pray that we will wake up. How many can relate?

The word of God takes us back to the first missionary journey of Paul and Barnabas (Acts 14:21–27). They proclaimed the good news about the risen Christ, made disciples of many despite threats to their own lives, encouraged these new disciples to stay true to their faith, established structures, and went back to report what God had done. The circle of disciples gets bigger and bigger, going from the Jews to the Gentiles.

Paul and Barnabas challenge us to live lives of integrity. They didn't compartmentalize their lives. For example, "Sunday we involve God, and Monday through Friday, we exclude God." Our personal and professional lives form a single whole life. We are called to live and act with integrity wherever we are and whatever our profession and relationships.

Life can't be divided into compartments. That was the *Titanic* mistake. When the *Titanic* set sail in 1912, it was declared unsinkable.

The ship's hull was divided into sixteen watertight compartments. Tragically, the *Titanic* sank. When the wreck was found in 1985, what they discovered was that damage to one compartment affected all the rest.

Many people make the *Titanic* mistake. But a person who tries to live a life of integrity, honesty, and truthfulness doesn't divide his/her life into compartments. We try always to be true to our inner best selves.

The author of the Acts may be asking whether we, like Paul and Barnabas, try to live lives of integrity.

In the book of Revelation, the author describes a visionary experience of the future in which he sees a new heaven and a new earth, a new Jerusalem, a universe in which we will experience the presence or glory of God. God will live in us, and we will live in God (Rv 21:1–5).

The author may be asking whether we're aware of God's presence in our lives.

The Gospel according to John takes us back to the farewell address of Jesus (Jn 13:31–35). Judas, the betrayer, has left the Passover meal. The die is cast: the arrest, trial, and execution are about to begin. The death/exaltation is near. Yes, Jesus will be lifted up on the cross, only to be lifted up into glory. And his message: "Love one another with the same self-sacrificing love I have shown you."

During this Easter season, we meet different biblical personalities: the questioning Thomas, the impulsive Peter, the purpose-driven Paul.

Today I would like to highlight Mary Magdalene, or Mary of Magdala. Mary is depicted in literature as a repentant prostitute. Daniel Brown's novel *The Da Vinci Code* depicts her as Jesus's wife. But Mary Magdalene was neither. She was from Magdala, near the Sea of Galilee. Luke's Gospel describes how Jesus exorcised from her seven demons. Tradition associates these with the seven deadly or capital sins: pride, avarice, gluttony, lust, jealousy, laziness, and anger. The poet Dante Alighieri describes these deadly attitudes in the concentric circles of the Inferno in his classic *The Divine Comedy*. So too does Chaucer in *The Canterbury Tales*. Their opposite are the seven heavenly virtues: living a life of dependency upon God, generosity, self-discipline, a chaste life, a simple life, a work ethic, and forgiveness.

Mary Magdalene and other biblical women supported Jesus. She was at the Crucifixion; she was the first witness of the empty tomb; she was the first to recognize Jesus in the garden. She is called by many "the apostle to the apostles" because she rushed to tell them the good news. She is a model of discipleship, inviting us to practice seven (another seven!) disciplines that will ignite a spark of light in us. These disciplines, all interconnected, will nurture our relationship with God.

1. Slow Down

Mother Teresa of Calcutta, of the Missionaries of Charity, explained, "In the silence of the heart God speaks. Learn to listen so that you will be able to speak to God. Listening and speaking is prayer." As a disciple of Jesus, it is so important to take at least ten minutes a day to tune into the presence of God. People find all sorts of ways to connect with God: a daily walk, a stop at a church, a quiet moment in the car. And there are all kinds of prayers and techniques that can bring us into the presence of God. One is breathing—inhaling God's presence in one breath, exhaling our worries in the next breath.

2. Serve Others

The Gospels are filled with examples of Jesus serving. We too are called to serve in our families, our workplaces, our local communities, and beyond. Engage, for example, in a parish volunteer ministry. Work at a soup kitchen, or St. Vincent de Paul, or Habitat for Humanity. Check the websites of Catholic Charities or the local Conference of Catholic Bishops for issues that need your support. And always remember: serving others begins in your own home, with compassion and forgiveness.

3. Study Wisdom

We should be lifelong learners. Study the Bible. Join our parish Bible study. And study the teachings of the church with a resource such as the *Catechism of the Catholic Church*. There are many resources (e.g., Formed.org).

4. Worship Together

Gather as often as you can with our faith community at St. Raphael to celebrate the presence of the risen Jesus, especially in our Eucharist where the living Christ presences himself to us sacramentally. The life of the triune God breathes within us, and we breathe within that life. And our liturgies nurture that relationship.

5. Share Your Faith with Others

Pope Francis challenges us to be missionary disciples. Faith sharing can be as simple as asking or reflecting with others on the work we do. How can we better reflect values or virtues, such as honesty, integrity, responsibility, friendship, courage, perseverance, compassion, loyalty, faith in God, and respect for colleagues?

6. Seek Counsel

Seek guidance from trusted friends in important matters so that you can make the right decision.

Guidance springs out of our relationship with God. God promises to guide those who walk with him. And never underestimate the common, sensible thing to do.

7. Travel Light

Ask yourself: do I really need this or that? Carry as little baggage as possible. Also do without other baggage: anger, impatience, selfishness, negative judgments, whatever might jeopardize your relationship with God.

These seven simple yet rigorous practices will help us keep the flame of faith alive. Faith is a gift, but, like a flower in a garden, it must be fed and cared for. These disciplines will nurture our relationship with God and keep faith alive so we will be a spark of light to others.

SIXTH SUNDAY OF EASTER

I was reading a story about Archbishop Fulton Sheen. A college student asked Sheen, "How did Jonah in the Bible manage to survive three days in the belly of a whale?" Sheen answered, "Frankly, I don't know, but when I get to heaven, I'll ask Jonah." The student shouted back, "Suppose Jonah didn't go to heaven." Fulton Sheen replied, "Then you ask him." The moral of the story: be careful how you ask a question.

The word of God takes us back to the beginnings of Christianity. Christianity then was not easily distinguishable from Judaism. In fact, many regarded Christianity simply as a new way of being Jewish. The question: do Christian non-Jews have to observe Jewish practices? (Acts 15:1–2, 22–29).

Paul and Barnabas discuss this with Peter and the other apostles in Jerusalem. How did they settle it? They compromise. Yes, these Gentile Christians should observe some Jewish practices so as not to scandalize their fellow disciples, but they don't have to observe all Jewish practices to be disciples of Jesus. Why? Because Jesus through his dying and rising reestablished our relationship with God. Jesus is indeed our way, our truth, and our life.

The author may be asking how we resolve tensions or conflicts in our lives. Love can only emerge if we forgive, work out compromises (i.e., be flexible), agree to disagree without being disagreeable, look for and compliment the good in one another, clarify our essential or core values, accept differences (i.e., our way isn't the only way), and communicate regularly.

Above all, good relationships demand that we distinguish between behavior and negative judgments. For example, *you're late for the birthday party* (behavior) versus *you're the most inconsiderate person I know* (negative judgment). Maybe there was an accident on the road, or there was another reason. Focus on the behavior and avoid negative judgments about behaviors in our relationships.

Like most things in life, we have to work at good relationships, sticking together especially through rough patches, with confidence that times will change and we'll reemerge closer.

The author of the book of Revelation describes a mystical experience in which he sees an awesome, dazzling new vision of reality, depicted as the new Jerusalem, built on the foundation of the apostles and radiating the glory or presence of God. The almighty God and the slain Lamb light up this vision (Rv 21:10–14, 22–23).

The author may be asking whether we recognize God's presence in our daily lives.

The Gospel according to John takes us back to the farewell address of Jesus at his Last Supper. In saying goodbye, Jesus considers how his community of disciples will continue after his departure. The disciples should be faithful to his words, especially his new commandment—to love one another. But this community will need guidance. So Jesus promises to send the Spirit, who will energize and guide them into the fullness of God's kingdom (Jn 14:23–29).

This Easter season, we have met different biblical personalities: Thomas, Peter, Paul, and Mary of Magdala. Today I would like to introduce Stephen.

Who was Stephen? He was a Spirit-filled leader in the Jerusalem church, a Greek-speaking Jewish Christian appointed, along with six others, to help needy widows. Stephen worked signs and wonders, proclaimed courageously that Jesus is the fulfillment of the messianic promises made to ancient Israel, had a visionary experience of the glory of God, outraged Jewish authorities with his so-called blasphemous claims about Jesus, and was dragged outside Jerusalem by a lynch mob and stoned to death. Stephen became the proto martyr of Christianity. His death was like that of Jesus. He forgave his executioners and cried out, "Lord Jesus, receive my spirit."

I believe Stephen had an intense relationship with God, nurtured through prayer.

But what is prayer? C.S. Lewis, the twentieth-century author and professor and theologian, wrote a series of letters titled *The Screwtape Letters*, between a senior devil, Screwtape, and an apprentice devil, Wormwood. Screwtape advises Wormwood how to win a soul for the devil. One method, Screwtape explains, is to create so much noise that men and women can no longer hear the voice of God. Does this ring true? We wake up to clock radios, watch TV at breakfast, listen to the car radio; check Facebook, Instagram, iPhones, e-mail, and so forth, all of which distract us from hearing God's voice in our lives. There's so much noise we can't hear ourselves think. The devil's strategy works.

For Jesus and the heroes and heroines of Christianity, prayer was their top priority. They prayed often and quietly to nurture their relationships with God. It's a two-way street.

Jesus of course is the model for prayer. He gives us some guidelines that in no way replace public worship. Here are some guidelines.

1. Keep it real.

Be genuine in your relationship with God. C.S. Lewis wrote, "The prayer preceding all prayers is, 'May it be the real "I" who speaks. May it be the real "Thou" that I speak to.'" Yes, our relationship with God has to be real, honest, and authentic.

2. Keep it quiet.

Jesus went up the mountain to pray. Find a place every day to pray without being distracted. Jesus encourages us to find time to be alone with God so that we can offload our guilt, our problems, and our worries.

3. Keep it simple.

Jesus admonishes us to keep our prayers simple. It is not the length that counts but the sincerity. Jesus also taught His disciples to be persistent in prayer, to go on asking, seeking, knocking. Our heavenly Father knows what we need.

There's a pattern to prayer as well, which Jesus taught us in the Our Father. Here's a paraphrase. We pray:

> Our Father: because we are sons and daughters of God, family members, heirs to the kingdom of God;
> Your name be honored and reverenced everywhere;
> May Your kingdom of truth and justice and peace and freedom permeate everyone;
> And may Your will be done on earth as it is in heaven.
> Satisfy our basic needs: food, health, home, a respectable livelihood, a good society in peace.
> Forgive us for the things we do wrong as we forgive those who wrong us.
> and protect us from the evil one (i.e., don't let us succumb to evils that will jeopardize our relationship with God).

This is the pattern of prayer Jesus gave us.

Finally, does God answer our prayers? Put simply: Yes but not always as we like. An anonymous verse shows how inventive God can be:

> I asked for strength, and God gave me difficulties to make me strong.
> I asked for wisdom, and God gave me problems to solve.
> I asked for prosperity, and God gave me a brain and the energy to work.
> I asked for courage, and God gave me dangers to overcome.
> I asked for love, and God gave me troubled people to help.
> I received nothing I wanted, but I received everything I needed.

Today the Spirit-filled Stephen invites us to pray, to converse with God as we would with a friend, a friendship based on love. May we nurture our friendship with God through daily prayer.

Seventh Sunday
of Easter (or Ascension)

There's plenty of excitement at the Kentucky Derby each May. It reminds me of the gambler who saw a priest blessing the forehead of a longshot horse lined up for a race. The horse surprisingly won. The priest kept blessing longshots on the forehead, and each won.

The gambler rushed to the ATM and withdrew all his savings for the last race. But this time, the priest blessed not the forehead but the eyes, ears, and hooves of the "old nag." The gambler bet all he had. When the horse came in last, the gambler was shocked. He asked the priest what happened. The priest answered, "I guess you can't tell the difference between a simple blessing and the last rites." Moral of the story: know your Catechism.

In May, we also celebrate Mother's Day. The words *mother* and *mom* evoke all kinds of images (e.g., homemaker, teacher, nurse, chauffeur). Whatever the job, a mother shows her children how to live. And the most important thing a mother can give? Unconditional love! Our mothers care, coach and mentor us, teach us, are patient and ready to listen. We can never measure the unconditional love, the unconditional acceptance, and the unconditional forgiveness of our mothers.

Yes, mothers are truly great teachers. Here are two things my mother taught me:

Logic. How many have heard their mom say, "Because I said so! That's why!"

And Mom taught about envy. She would say, "Millions of less fortunate kids don't have the wonderful parents you do!"

Do these lessons sound familiar? Thank you, mothers, for all you do for us.

During these forty-some days, we celebrate the Paschal Mystery of Jesus Christ: his death and resurrection, his ascension to his Father in glory, the descent of the Spirit of God upon the disciples.

The death, resurrection, ascension, and descent are different aspects of the one Paschal Mystery, the passage of Jesus from this earthly life through death into a new, transfigured, heavenly reality—and the risen Christ anticipates our own future.

Jesus has been appearing suddenly—appearing in glory—and then disappearing.

The ascension that we celebrate today is Jesus's final leave-taking so something new can happen: the descent of the Spirit of God on Pentecost. Yes, the living Christ stays among us, ever active through the power of the Spirit.

The ascension connects the Gospel of Luke and the book of the

Acts. The Gospel signals the close of Jesus's earthy ministry, and Acts heralds the beginning of the church's ministry, proclaiming the good news that Jesus is alive and that because Jesus lives, we live.

Paul in his letter prays that we will grow in wisdom and enlightenment so that we will see more clearly God's saving work in Jesus Christ.

Jesus is indeed the head of the church, the mystical Body of Christ, the people of God, the herald of the good news, the servant called to wash the feet of our fellow human beings.

In the Gospel according to Luke, Jesus tells the disciples they are eye witnesses to the death and resurrection, that they are to proclaim this good news to all people, and that he will send the promise of God, the Spirit, to the disciples so that they can continue Jesus's saving ministry until he comes again to transform this universe into a new, indescribable reality. And then Jesus was taken up into heaven. The disciples were filled with hope for the Spirit (Lk 24:46–53).

That's my theme for today: hope. Hope is a confident anticipation of something yet to come. Pope Benedict XVI captured its meaning magnificently in his encyclical *Saved by Hope*. This hope looks forward to seeing God as God really is—face-to-face.

Hope looks for the good in people, instead of harping on the worst.

Hope discovers what can be done instead of grumbling about what cannot.

Hope pushes forward when it would be easy to quit.

History is filled with people who held on to hope. One of my favorites is Helen Keller, writer, lecturer, and inspiration to many of us. She said, "No pessimist ever discovered the secrets of the stars or sailed to an unchartered land or opened a new haven to the human spirit." Keller overcame physical obstacles that most of us can't imagine. How? She possessed a positive spirit that helped her discover a world of possibilities. We too, with a positive can-do spirit, can discover a similar world of possibilities.

Hope points us to the future. We are fascinated with the future. What will the future be like? Everywhere, we see change: political, economic, scientific, and religious. The Internet immediately put us in touch with people from all over the world. People want to know what will happen before it actually happens.

Sometimes we may not like what is unfolding. How to react to the shape of things? Some rebel, while others despair or withdraw. But what is the Christian response? Hope. We are forever seeking to go beyond the here and now, to dream the impossible dream. We want to reach beyond ourselves for that which is to come. Some of you may hope that I will end this homily soon so that you can get on with today's activities.

The point is, for many philosophers, hope best expresses what human existence is all about. Images of hope weave in and out of the Hebrew and Christian scriptures. Initially, the hopes of the ancient Hebrews were very concrete: land, sons and daughters, peace and prosperity. And when finally their hopes were dashed with the fall of the Southern Kingdom in the sixth century BC, God began to build up new and better hopes for them—a Messianic era, a Messiah who would rescue them.

The New Testament is rooted and grounded in Jesus of Nazareth. He is our hope. At the very core of Christianity is the central reality that Jesus appeared alive to the disciples after his death. There were many appearances. God by the power of the Spirit transformed the earthly Jesus into a heavenly Jesus. The risen Christ anticipates God's future for all of us. By virtue of baptism, we experience the beginnings of that future—life with God forever.

Christian hope is the conviction that the universe in which we live has an ultimate purpose, that Christ in his Second Coming will bring to completion the process of transformation inaugurated by his resurrection. This hope challenges us to do everything we can to usher in that future: to advocate peace, compassion, generosity, forgiveness, and fairness. Above all, this hope challenges all of us to reach out to that which alone is of everlasting value—the human person.

In the end, all Christian hope will be realized when the risen Christ, by the power of the Spirit, hands over the universe at the end of time to his heavenly Father.

May God fill us with Christian hope this Ascension Day and every day of our lives.

PENTECOST SUNDAY

Many schools are beginning to wind down the academic year. Summer is almost upon us. Before then, teachers have to grade their students. Uneasy is the relationship between teacher and student. Which reminds me of a story about Jesus, rabbi and teacher, and his disciples.

When Jesus took his twelve disciples up the mountain and gathered them together, he taught them, saying, "Blessed are they who recognize their absolute dependency upon God ... Blessed are they who hunger and thirst for God ... Blessed are the merciful ... Blessed are the peacemakers."

Then Peter said, "Do we have to write this down?" Andrew asked, "Are we supposed to know this?" James wondered, "Will we have a test?" The relationship between teacher and student is uneasy.

Today we celebrate Pentecost, the outpouring of the Spirit upon the disciples centuries ago. Pentecost concludes the Easter season and begins the mission of the church, the people of God, to continue the saving work of Jesus Christ until he comes again in power and glory at the end-time to bring to completion the process of transformation inaugurated by his resurrection.

And you and I can continue that work by awakening within ourselves the seven gifts or energies of the Spirit already in us: wisdom to focus on what truly matters, our relationship with God and one another; understanding and knowledge, to enter deeply into the mysteries of God and the truths of faith; counsel to make good moral decisions; fortitude to stand up for what is right; piety to give God who created us our praise and worship; and finally fear of the Lord, the healthy concern never to lose our friendship with God.

The word "Pentecost" comes from a Greek word meaning "fiftieth," the fiftieth day after the Passover. The Hebrews initially celebrated this festival after harvesting the spring wheat in their fields. Later they associated it with the covenant God made with their forebears on Mt. Sinai—a covenant summed up simply yet powerfully in that simple phrase: "You are my people, and I am your God."

In the Christian tradition, Pentecost celebrates an aspect of the Paschal Mystery, which includes the death, resurrection, ascension, and the descent of the Spirit upon the disciples.

The book of Acts describes how the Jews had come to Jerusalem to celebrate Pentecost. And suddenly the Spirit—described in images of wind and fire (images that symbolize power and energy and vitality)— was poured out on the disciples and fired them up to proclaim the Gospel courageously throughout the Mediterranean (Acts 2:1–11).

The word of God asks you and me, do we try to stand up for what is true, right, and good? I always remember a great quotation: "If not you, who? If not now, when?"

The letter of Paul to the Christian community at Corinth in Greece speaks about all the different gifts the Spirit bestows upon us—all for the greater common good, the community. In this age of individualism, where we often overemphasize the individual at the expense of the greater common good, Paul's words are a powerful challenge.

In the Gospel according to John, the author describes a post-resurrection appearance of Jesus where he breathes upon the disciples (as God breathed life into man in the second chapter of Genesis) and in that gesture bestows the Spirit upon them (Jn 14:15–16, 23b–26).

Now and then, I like to see a good classic movie—for example, Alfred Hitchcock's *North by Northwest,* Fellini's *La Dolce Vita,* Kubrick's *2001: A Space Odyssey,* Cameron's *Titanic,* and Orson Welles's *Citizen Kane.* Last week, I came across a movie titled *Zelig.* Leonard Zelig, the main character, has no personality of his own; he assumes whatever personalities he meets. He's forever changing his color, accent, shape. He has no ideas or opinions of his own; he simply conforms. He wants to fit in, to be accepted, to be liked. For a while, Zelig's transformations make him a sensation: New York City welcomes him with confetti and ticker tape. He's famous for being a nobody. Eventually he begins to see himself for what he is: a disturbed person looking for identity, looking for his true self. He's dissatisfied with being a nobody.

But Pentecost proclaims that we are somebody. We have an identity by virtue of the life-giving waters of baptism. We are sons and daughters of God our Father, called to live a life worthy of our calling and heirs to the kingdom of God. We are living temples of God, alive with the life of the triune God.

What does it mean to be alive? What does it mean to be alive in Christ? How really alive in Christ are we?

First, what makes you feel alive? Experiencing the awesomeness of Niagara Falls or the Grand Canyon? Watching a space shuttle lift off? Watching your favorite team win an exciting game? Hearing Justin Bieber or Jimmy Fallon or Taylor Swift? Holding a baby in your arms? Accomplishing a challenging task at work? Any of these experiences, and many more, can make us feel alive.

Pablo Casals, the great cellist-conductor, experienced at age ninety severe arthritis and emphysema. Each morning began with agony. Casals would shuffle, badly stooped. But when he sat to play Bach or Brahms, his body slowly came alive with music. Afterward, he would walk with no trace of a shuffle, eat heartily, talk animatedly, and then walk on the beach. He felt alive. Music energized him.

What energizes you and me?

Second, what does it mean to be alive in Christ? We are gifted with God's triune life in baptism, our initiation rite into a community of disciples. In early Christianity, candidates for baptism were often immersed in a pool of water. When the candidate stepped down into the water and came up on the other side, that gesture symbolized a dying to a self-centered life and a rising to a God-centered life.

Baptism makes us alive in Christ. At birth, we lack a relationship with God. That's what original sin means—a lack of relationship with God. The book of Genesis describes this. In the beginning, man and woman walked with God. They had friendship with God and one another. Somehow, they lost that friendship; they fell from grace. They hid from God, man blamed woman, and the earthly elements worked against them. So God became flesh in Jesus. That reconnected us to the triune God. And through the waters of baptism, we enter into this community, this fellowship of grace. We are alive in Christ.

And last, how really alive in Christ are we? The Spirit of God is within us. That Spirit calls us to continue the saving work of Jesus Christ. We are indeed his "hands and feet and eyes and ears and voice." And the Spirit of God empowers us to mirror or reflect the fruits of the Spirit in our daily lives: love, joy, peace, patience, kindness, goodness, faithfulness, gentleness, and self-control. We are alive with the life of the triune God—that is the lesson of Pentecost. Let that life of God breathe in us every day of our lives.

THE MOST HOLY TRINITY SUNDAY

C hildren have lively images of God. How many remember a paperback titled *Dear God: Children's Letters to God?* I think of letters such as:

> Dear God, Thank you for my parents, my sister Anita, and for my grandma and grandpa. I forgive you for my brother Phil. I guess you didn't finish working on him.

One of my favorite stories is about children lined up in the school cafeteria. At the beginning of the line was a pile of apples. A teacher posted a note on the apple tray: "Take *only one*. God is watching." At the other end of the line, there was a table with a pile of chocolate-chip cookies. And a youngster wrote a note: "Take all you want. God is watching the apples." Yes, children do have lively imaginations about God.

Today we celebrate the feast of the triune God, the fundamental and distinctive truth of Christianity. That is why we begin every liturgy "In the name of the Father and the Son and the Holy Spirit" and are sent forth with the blessing of the "Father, Son, and Holy Spirit."

There's a remarkable prayer popularized in the Broadway musical *Godspell:* "Day by day, oh, dear Lord, three things I pray: To see thee more clearly: Love thee more dearly: Follow thee more nearly, day by day." Would that we could make that prayer a reality.

Now when we hear the word "God," what do we immediately think of? A God of do's and don'ts? Thunder and lightning?

The Bible, our privileged book, gives us many splendid images of God. The Hebrew scriptures speak of God as a walking companion, a God as tender as a mother. "Can a mother forget her child? And even if she should ... I will never forget you." These scriptures also speak of a God who wants to share his wisdom with us. In the New Testament, the image of God in the parables of the good shepherd and the prodigal son are balanced with the image of God in the parable of the last judgment. Yes, there are many splendid images, but all these images cannot capture fully the inexhaustible reality of God.

The nineteenth-century author Henry David Thoreau wrote that "the mass of men lead lives of quiet desperation." This celebrated quote penned over 150 years ago rings true today for too many people. Ask yourself: are folks so often caught up in the hustle and bustle of daily life that they easily forget what they're here for, the purpose of life?

No human relationship can completely satisfy us. That's why St Augustine wrote in his autobiographical *Confessions*, "Thou hast made us for Yourself, O God, and our hearts are restless until they find rest in You." Yes, we were born to live in a relationship with God—the triune God—and that's what today's feast highlights.

So, what does the word of God have to say to us today? That word takes us back to the wisdom literature of ancient Israel, the book of Proverbs. The author personifies wisdom as a woman, as creative energy, as a playful companion of God who witnesses the mighty acts of God in this multi universe of ours (Prv 8:22–31).

The early Christians saw Jesus in this wisdom image, the Word made flesh among us. And today we pray for the wisdom to know what truly matters in life, to distinguish the important from the unimportant.

Paul, in his letter to the Christian community at Rome, waxes eloquently about the saving work of Jesus Christ. Through him we have a right relationship with God, and the essence of that relationship is the practice of the virtues of faith or trust in God, hope or the anticipation of something yet to come, and love or giving until there is nothing left to give (Rom 5:1–5).

We pray today that God will strengthen our relationship with right faith, firm hope, perfect love.

In the Gospel according to John, Jesus in his farewell alludes to the mystery of the triune God: The Spirit that comes through Jesus and the Father will guide our global Catholic community of disciples into all truth. Today we pray the Spirit of truth will guide us (Jn 16:12–15).

The mystery of the triune God (a God who is one yet distinctive in modalities or "persons," Father, Son, and Spirit; neither is the other; a God who is love) invites us to reflect upon our own relationship with God and one another. I like to think most people do have a relationship with God, perhaps more subconscious than conscious. Why? Because we are forever trying to make better sense out of our lives, trying to find answers, especially in moments of crisis—for example, the death of a parent, spouse, or child, a broken marriage, loss of a job, misunderstandings, and so forth. In moments such as these, people often ask the most fundamental questions of human life. What is the purpose of my life? Where is my life going? These are religious questions, questions we cannot help but try to answer.

As we go through the cycle of our own human development, adolescence to young adulthood, middle years to old age, we are forever trying to better integrate our lives or get our act together, so to speak.

When we are young, we have so many hopes, so many dreams. The world is our oyster, so to speak. As we move through the middle years, we may not be as dreamy eyed. We want to live for something greater than ourselves, something that gives ultimate meaning. But at times, we begin to wonder. We accomplished so little, and now it is almost over. What was it all about?

Life seems to be marred by too many mindless tragedies: violence, international threats, natural disasters.

But then again at other moments, we have experiences that lift us up out of our routine—moments that make us wonder. A starry sky, the joy of friendship, the golden rays of a sunset, the accomplishment of a goal. Such experiences can take us out of ourselves and into the presence of an awesome power beyond us. We begin to experience the transcendent dimension of our own lives.

Yes, we say, there must be a power beyond us, a purposeful and gracious God who is responsible not only for this magnificent universe but also for our very lives.

Catholic Christianity says that this is indeed a gracious God who can heal the brokenness of human life. Yes, this God became flesh in Jesus and is alive among us by the power of the Spirit. That is the mystery of the triune God, a God who is one in three: Father, Son, and Spirit.

This is the same God who freed the Hebrews from their oppressors in ancient Egypt, who renewed his covenant with them at Sinai. This God showed his face to us in Jesus of Nazareth. In and through him, we live in God's triune life, and the triune God lives in us.

And this triune God, the model of self-giving love, empowers us to reach out in love to one another with compassion, forgiveness, a smile, a kind word, a helping hand. And in reaching out to one another in love, we become like the triune God in their self-giving love.

THE BODY AND BLOOD OF CHRIST

D id you hear about Moses, Jesus, and God the Father on a golf course? Moses teed off first, and the ball landed in the water. Moses parted the water and hit the ball in for a birdie. Jesus teed off next, the ball landed in the water, and Jesus walked on the water and hit a birdie. Lastly, God the Father teed off. Before the ball hit the water, a fish jumped up and caught the ball. Then an eagle caught the fish. Lightning struck, the eagle dropped the fish, and the fish dropped the ball for a hole in one.

Jesus turned to God the Father and said, "Dad, if you don't quit playing like that, we're not playing with you anymore."

My own golf game is summed up in this prayer: "God grant me the serenity to accept the shots I miss, the courage to try, try again, and the wisdom not to throw my clubs in the lake."

This weekend, we honor our fallen soldiers in memorial services. In the great conflicts in which our nation has fought, the total number of slain is truly staggering. Just counting the Revolutionary War, Civil War, World Wars I and II, Korea, Vietnam, Iraq, and Afghanistan, more than 1.2 million Americans died for the freedoms we enjoy.

In 1863, Abraham Lincoln captured the sacredness of all battlefields when he told a crowd at the Gettysburg cemetery, "We cannot dedicate, we cannot consecrate, we cannot hallow this ground. The brave soldiers, living and dead, who struggled here, have consecrated it far above our poor power to add or detract."

I invite all of us to pray that our fallen soldiers have an eternal dwelling place with God.

Today we celebrate the Feast of Corpus Christi, the Body and Blood of Christ.

How often have we heard the question, what are we doing for dinner? Grilling? Getting a pizza or a Chinese takeout? Then the follow-up question, will we sit down as a family or eat and run?

Jesus invites us to participate in a sacrificial meal of thanksgiving for the gift of God's eternal life through the death and resurrection of Jesus, a meal in which the bread and wine become the body and blood of the risen Christ to nourish the life of God already in us. Yes, the risen Christ is truly present in the bread and wine.

The word of God takes us back almost four thousand years to a mysterious kingly figure in the book of Genesis, Melchizedek. He blesses Abram for winning a decisive battle over the Canaanites. They celebrate with bread and wine (Gn 14:18–20).

This biblical story, for some, prefigures the Lord's Supper.

Paul, in his letter to the Christian community at Corinth in Greece, highlights the sacredness of the Lord's Supper. Unfortunately, the gathering before the Lord's Supper was getting out of hand. Some Corinthians were showing up drunk or getting drunk; others weren't sharing the food/drink they brought.

So Paul reminds them, "This sacrificial meal reenacts the life-giving death/resurrection of Jesus, the new and everlasting covenant God made with us through the death/resurrection of Jesus by the power of the Spirit." It is, Paul emphasizes, a truly sacred experience that should be celebrated reverently (1 Cor 11:23–26).

This Lord's Supper quickly developed into the structure we know today: the Liturgy of the Word and the Liturgy of the Eucharist. Herein, we worship and praise God for who he is and what he has done for us.

In the Gospel according to Luke, Jesus satisfies the hungry crowd in the so-called miracle of the multiplication of the loaves and fish. People have so many hungers. Some hunger for bread; others for justice and freedom; and still others for peace. Jesus here satisfies the crowd's physical hunger, but this wonder prefigures the liturgy of the Eucharist where the bread and wine become the body and blood of the risen Christ, satisfying our spiritual hunger (Lk 9:11–17).

To understand today's liturgy of the Eucharist, we have to go back to Jesus's Last Supper in Jerusalem. When Jesus sat down to his Last Supper, he faced three challenges.

First, Jesus had to leave us, and yet he wanted to stay with us. How did Jesus solve this? Listen to his words: "This is my body; this is my blood." The bread and wine look and feel and taste like bread and wine, but they are not. The bread and wine become the real presence of the risen Christ.

The second challenge Jesus faced was he wanted to die for each one of us, and yet he could die only once as a human being. How did Jesus solve this? Listen to his words: "Do this in memory of me." The same victim who was crucified once outside Jerusalem centuries ago returns whenever we celebrate the liturgy of the Eucharist.

The third challenge was that Jesus wanted to be one with us, and yet this was impossible this side of heaven. How did Jesus solve this challenge? Listen to his words: "Take and eat; take and drink." Jesus invites us to become one with him in Communion.

These were the three ways in which Jesus solved the challenges he faced at his Last Supper:

He had to leave us, and yet he wanted to stay, so He left us and stays: the bread and wine become the real presence of the risen Christ.

He wanted to die for each one of us and yet could die but once as a human being, so the Victim (the lamb, the sacrifice) returns to us today and every day in the liturgy of the Eucharist.

He wanted to be one with us and yet couldn't this side of heaven, so he gave us the next best thing: Communion.

What is the purpose of the bread we eat? The blood we drink? To form us into a faith community. Paul wrote, "Because the bread is one, we, though many, are one body." This bread we eat and this blood we drink should not only form us into a more loving faith community but also should empower us to reach out compassionately (with our time and talent especially) to the people around us in our community.

The Liturgy of the Word/Eucharist is indeed a family meal; the triune God and we participate in a sacrificial meal. Perhaps this should be our prayer:

Bless this faith family of yours, O God, as we journey
toward our eternal dwelling place.
May you always remind us of the strength we have when
we stand together,
united in faith, hope, and love with you, O God.
Help us, O God, to open our hearts to one another,
to listen when one of us is crying out,
to extend a helping hand when one of us is hurting,
to rejoice when one of us has cause for celebration.
O God, we are united forever with you by our heavenly
family ties.
We pray that we will never take that for granted
and that we always will live in your presence, Father,
Son, and Holy Spirit.
Amen.

Tenth Sunday in Ordinary Time

I read about a Mississippi judge who was asked to take a stand on whiskey in the 1920s when Prohibition was a controversial issue. The judge began, "If when you say whiskey, you mean the devil's brew, the scourge of society, the curse of family life, then I am against it." However, he countered, "If when you say whiskey, you mean the oil of conversation, the glow of warmth among friends, and so on, then I am for it. This is my stand. I will not retreat from it. I will not compromise." Now that's what I would call straddling-the-fence politics in the good ole days. And some think it hasn't changed that much today.

Let me begin with a story about two men, seriously ill, occupying a hospital room. One man was allowed to sit up in bed for an hour each day to help drain fluid from his lungs. The other had to stay flat on his back. The two would talk for hours on end about families, jobs, sports, and so on.

Every afternoon when the man by the window could sit up, he would describe to his roommate all he could see: the park with a lovely lake; ducks and swans, children sailing their model boats; young lovers walking arm in arm among the colorful flowers. As he described all this in exquisite detail, the other man would close his eyes and imagine these scenes, which enlivened his days.

When the man by the window died, the other man asked if he could be moved next to the window. The nurse happily obliged and then left. The man slowly propped himself up to take his first look at the world outside, only to discover the bed faced a blank wall.

He asked the nurse how his roommate could describe such wonderful things. The nurse responded that the man was blind and couldn't even see the wall. She said, "Perhaps he just wanted to encourage you." The point is one can be incredibly happy making others happy, despite one's own situation. And that's what Elijah and Jesus did in today's word of God; they were happy making two widows happy.

The word of God takes us back in our imaginations almost three thousand years to what we know today as Lebanon. Elijah means "my God is Yahweh." And Elijah lived up to that name. In this passage, a struggling, poor single mom is grieving over the death of her only child. She's angry with God and takes her anger out on Elijah (1 Kgs 17:17–24).

I couldn't help but think of the recent iconic news image of the three-year-old Syrian boy whose body washed up on the beach in Turkey, and the unspeakable grief of his father, who also lost his wife and another toddler.

But in the book of Kings, Elijah pleads with God to bring back to life the widow's child. And lo and behold, the widow's grief turns into joy. She recognizes the compassionate power of God in her life. The author may be asking us, do we recognize God's compassionate power in our lives?

Paul, in his letter to the Christian community in Galatia (what we know as central Turkey), speaks about his vocation in life. He once savagely persecuted Christians—until he experienced the power of the risen Christ on his way to Damascus in Syria. That awesome and overwhelming experience turned Paul's life upside down. He became a passionate evangelizer, a fiery preacher of the Gospel—the good news that Jesus, once crucified and now risen, is alive, and because he lives, we live (Gal 1:11–19).

Paul may be asking us how passionate are we about witnessing to Gospel virtues in our lives.

In the Gospel according to Luke, the author describes the widow of Nain who has just lost her only son. Jesus was deeply touched by her grief. He raised the young man to life. The crowd is awed because it is a sign that a great prophet is in their midst. Jesus became a sign of hope (Lk 7:11–17).

The author may be asking us: is the Risen Christ a sign of hope for us?

I always wondered if those two sons changed their lives dramatically when they came back to life. They seemed to have had a second chance.

But we only get one life. We might wish for more. The celebrated twentieth-century British author D.H. Lawrence wrote in a letter, "If only one could have two lives. The first in which to make one's mistakes... and the second in which to profit by them." That line is paraphrased beautifully in the film *The Natural* with Robert Redford and Glenn Close.

There are no dress rehearsals for life; we are on stage immediately. But the good news is this: even if we make mistakes, we can still make something out of the rest of our lives, with God's grace.

To paraphrase chapter 12 of Paul's letter to the Romans: make a new start; be transformed; live a holy life; please God; get rid of the rubbish in your life; hate what is evil; cling to what is good; be hospitable; be sincere in your love; be joyful in hope; be generous; be patient in adversities; and be faithful in prayer. What a splendid guide about how to make something out of the rest of our lives!

Yes, make the most of each day. We might begin with Romans or the beatitudes. For example,

> If you're a parent working to pay the bills, but making
> time to be with your children when they need you,
> blessed are you. Heaven will be yours.

If you are overwhelmed by the care of a dying spouse, a sick child or an elderly parent but you try your best to make a loving home for them, blessed are you. One day your sorrow will be transformed into joy.

If you happily give your time to work at a soup kitchen, shop for a housebound neighbor, help a youngster with a classroom assignment; if you befriend the uncool, the unpopular, the perpetually lost, blessed are you. Count God among your friends.

If you refuse to take shortcuts when it comes to doing what is right, if you refuse to compromise your integrity and ethics, if you refuse to take refuge in the rationalization that "everybody does it," blessed are you. You will triumph.

If you readily spend time listening and consoling others who looks to you for support, for guidance, for compassion; if you manage to heal wounds and build bridges; if others see in you goodness, graciousness, joy and serenity; if you can see the good in everyone and seek the good for everyone, blessed are you. You are nothing less than the face of God in our midst.

Yes, make the best out of the rest of your life. I don't know what the two sons in today's word of God did, but we can begin today to make the best out of the rest of our lives, with God's grace.

ELEVENTH SUNDAY
IN ORDINARY TIME

I was at an abbey this week and heard a story about one of the early abbots who was dying. All the monks were gathered around his bedside. One of the monks gave the abbot a glass of milk with lots of brandy in it, to ease his pain. The abbot took a sip and suddenly perked up. One of the monks finally asked for the abbot's dying words. The abbot took another big gulp of the brandy-soaked milk, smiled, and said, "Don't ever sell that cow." I couldn't find the cow!

I begin with a story related to today's word of God. In 1972, the *Washington Post* printed a photo of a young Vietnamese girl running on a road, arms outstretched, clothes burnt off, skin blackened by napalm, screaming in agony. That iconic photo symbolized, for many, the worst of the Vietnam War.

After fourteen months in the hospital and seventeen operations, the girl, named Kim, returned home, worried that her scars were so ugly that no one would want to marry her.

Some years later, she read the New Testament for the first time and became a Christian. She said, "It was the fire of the bomb that burned my body, and it was the skill of the doctor that mended my skin, but it took the power of God to heal my heart."

Kim eventually became a medical doctor, married, escaped from Vietnam, and lives in Canada.

She agreed to speak in Washington, DC, on Veteran's Day in 1996, before a crowd. She spoke briefly and movingly. "I have suffered a lot from both physical and emotional pain. Sometimes I thought I could not live, but God saved my life and gave me faith and hope."

Kim then uttered healing words of grace and forgiveness: "Even if I could talk face-to-face with the pilot who dropped the bomb, I would tell him we can't change history, but we should try to do good things for the present and for the future to promote peace." The veterans in the crowd broke into an explosion of applause.

One man rushed to a security officer with a note, asking him to deliver it to Kim. "I'm the man you are looking for," the note read. Asked if she was willing to see him, she said, "Yes." Kim looked into the man's eyes and extended the same arms she had raised as she ran in agony from the bomb. She hugged the man, and he began to sob. "I'm so sorry. I'm just so sorry," he said. "It is okay. I forgive. I forgive," she said, echoing her favorite Bible verse, "Forgive, and you will be forgiven."

A new photo of a young Vietnamese mother embracing an ex-soldier supplanted the infamous photo of a terrified little girl fleeing the napalm bomb. Her words and that striking new photo symbolize for me the meaning of forgiveness in today's word of God, which takes us back to the tenth century before Jesus (the 900s) to King David in Jerusalem. God had super-blessed David. But David wasn't grateful. One day, David sees a beautiful married woman by the name of Bathsheba, bathing on her terrace. Lust got the better of him, and Bathsheba became pregnant. To make matters worse, David engineered the death of Bathsheba's husband. David abused his power, as some public officials today abuse theirs.

David then marries Bathsheba, and she bears him a son. But David realizes, through the prophet Nathan, how wrong this was and asks God's forgiveness. God always forgives, if we're truly sorry, no matter how far we stray from God (2 Sm 12:7–10, 13).

The author of the book of Samuel may be asking, do we ask for the forgiveness of one another when we're truly sorry for wronging them?

Paul, in his letter to the Christian community in Galatia, Turkey, proclaims that through the gift of God's grace, we have a relationship or friendship with God. We cannot earn God's grace. God's life is a gift that is ours though the death and resurrection of Jesus by the power of the Spirit, a gift initially bestowed upon us in the life-giving waters of baptism. In Jesus Christ, we belong to God and one another in the Mystical Body of Christ (Gal 2:16, 19–21).

Paul may be asking us whether we recognize that we are one human family, brothers and sisters to one another, with God as our Father and with responsibilities to reach out compassionately to one another.

In the Gospel according to Luke, chapter 7, the author tells the story of the penitent woman at the house of a Pharisee who invited Jesus to dine with him. The author doesn't name the woman; she's simply a sinner. And the woman anoints the feet of Jesus and wipes them dry with her hair.

And the Pharisee (incredibly self-righteous) silently condemns Jesus for not divining who this woman is. But Jesus reads his thoughts.

So Jesus proposes a parable of debtors. Which one loved the creditor more, the one who owed five hundred coins or fifty? Jesus forgives the woman and welcomes her as a friend.

That is the theme that emerges in today's word of God: forgiveness.

A primary characteristic of discipleship is forgiveness. There's a folk wisdom that says "forgive and forget." But sometimes we can't forgive wrongs unless we remember! An injury done. A broken relationship. Perhaps we even contributed to the wrong.

Maybe you have even heard someone say, "I will never forgive him/her for what they have done to me." In moments like that, we have to forgive ourselves as well as the people who injured us.

In his book titled *The Chief: A Memoir of Fathers and Sons*, former *Time* magazine writer Lance Morrow noted, "Not to forgive is to be imprisoned by the past, by old grievances that do not permit us to move forward with our own lives. Not to forgive is to give oneself to another's control...to be locked into a sequence of outrage and revenge. Forgiveness frees the forgiver to move forward with his or her life."

Forgiveness is the conscious decision to let go of the anger and resentment toward someone who has hurt us. I emphasize it's an act of the will. Forgiving the person does not mean I have to forget. The decision to forgive does not imply that I condone or excuse what the person did. It does not even demand that the one who offended me is sorry or repents, although forgiveness is more difficult in these cases.

Forgiveness is my decision. Letting go is never easy. But it is part of the death that precedes resurrection.

Our faith helps us to realize that we are children of the same God.

God loves us unconditionally. If only we could see as God sees. God can see good in the offender even if we can't. I think of how parents love their children unconditionally, even children who deeply aggrieved them. How much more must our heavenly Father love all of us unconditionally.

Yes, the word of God invites us to forgive. God asks us to forgive ourselves and to forgive others, to participate in his gift of forgiveness.

I pray that God will give all of us the grace to participate in the forgiveness of the risen Christ, so that we can be at peace with ourselves and one another, as true disciples of Jesus.

TWELFTH SUNDAY
IN ORDINARY TIME

F or Father's Day, many of us can think of humorous stories about our fathers. My father was always shopping for a bargain. When we were youngsters, he took me and my brothers shopping for our Christmas and Easter suits. One day, with the three of us in tow, he said to the salesman, "I want to see the cheapest suit in the store," and the salesman looked him in the eye and said, "You're wearing it."

The word "father" or "dad" evokes many images. When I think of my own father, I think of certain qualities he possessed in abundance (qualities that all good fathers possess): love (he tried to do his best for us), commitment (he stuck by us), support (he gave as much as he could), forgiveness (he wasn't afraid to say he's sorry), communication (he listened to us, especially around the dinner table), spirituality (we always went to church on Sundays), we spent time together, and he had a good sense of humor.

The word of God takes us back in our imaginations to the sixth century before Jesus (the 500s) to a man named Zechariah, one of the twelve minor prophets. He contrasts grief and joy, judgment and salvation. The author here describes a future in which God will pour out his grace upon the Hebrews, disillusioned and demoralized back in their homeland after their exile in Babylonia. But first they must ask God's forgiveness for killing this mysterious "servant." The early Christian community saw in this not so easily understandable passage the Messiah, the crucified Jesus, with a lance thrust into his side. This image of Jesus symbolizes a fountain from which flows forgiveness and grace and salvation (Zec 12:10–11; 13:1).

Paul, in his Letter to the Christian community in Galatia, proclaims that we, through the gift of faith in Jesus Christ and the waters of baptism, have become sons and daughters of God our Father. We are covered in Christ (i.e., called to reveal the glory or presence of God in our lives). We belong to the risen Christ, and just as God transformed Jesus into a new heavenly reality, so too will God transform us into a new heavenly reality, which St. Paul centuries ago described so splendidly: no eye has seen, no ear has heard what God has prepared for those who love him (Gal 3:26–29).

In the Gospel according to Luke, Jesus asks the disciples, "Who am I?" And Peter answers, "You are the Messiah, the anointed one, the "Christos." "But this Messiah," Jesus says, "is a suffering Messiah who through his death and resurrection will open up to all human beings a future beyond this earthly life." And just as this Messiah suffered, so too we may have to suffer—in other words, take up our crosses, whether it's sickness, misunderstanding, loss, whatever, and follow the suffering Messiah so that we too can enter into glory (Lk 9:18–24).

What caught my eye in today's word of God was Paul's letter to the Galatians, which highlights our dignity as new creatures, sons and daughters of God our Father and heirs to the kingdom of God. In Genesis, chapter 1, we read that God created us in his own image. Every human being has an innate dignity, Paul proclaims loudly and clearly.

I would like to tell you about a twentieth-century man who took a heroic swing for human dignity. He broke baseball's color barrier. The film *42: The Jackie Robinson Story* is about the player and the baseball owner who changed baseball—and America—forever. The movie is a great lesson on segregation in the South prior to the civil rights movement.

Born in 1919 to Georgia sharecroppers (I invite you to read John Steinbeck's *The Grapes of Wrath* for a glimpse into the life of a sharecropper), Jackie Robinson and his siblings were raised by a single mom who worked as a housekeeper to support the family.

Jackie, who grew up to be a college graduate and a decorated army officer in WWII, was a talented shortstop in the Negro National League. Branch Rickey, owner of the Brooklyn Dodgers, my hometown, was convinced the time had come to bring a Negro player through the farm system into the big leagues. Rickey claimed he was doing it for business—to get more African Americans in the park—but he later revealed to Robinson the real reason: he'd decided to take on the baseball establishment. The Dodgers scouted prospects, and Robinson was drafted and made his Major League debut in 1947.

Rickey had no illusions about the controversy this would generate and cautioned the young player that he would have to temper his fierce pride. Robinson asked Rickey, "You want a player who doesn't have the guts to fight back?"

"No," Rickey replied, "I want a player who's got the guts *not* to fight back." Rickey continued, "People are not going to like this. They'll do anything to get you to react. Echo a curse, and they'll hear only yours. Follow a blow with a blow, and they'll say, 'The Negro lost his temper.' Your enemy will be out in full force, and you cannot meet him on his own low ground. We win with hitting, running, fielding—only that. We win if the world is convinced of two things: that you are a gentleman and a great baseball player." Jackie Robinson shattered baseball's color barrier by competing with skill and treating his teammates and fans with respect.

He often told audiences, "A life isn't important except in the impact it has on others." And throughout his life, he believed "the richest treasure anybody has is his/her dignity." Robinson exemplified character. And that's what St. Paul challenges us to become in light of our innate dignity.

Character defines who we are, at the core of our innermost selves. A person of moral character will choose fair-mindedness over bigotry, the dignity of the person over impersonal business or material advantage, respect for human beings over the lust for pleasure, or power, or personal success, a willingness to go the extra mile to make something "just right" because it's the better and worthy thing to do.

People of character will speak up for what is right and defend what is just. They will take a stand on principle and conscience—yes, an informed conscience—even if it is to one's worldly disadvantage, even if others turn against them. A person of character will show courage and not simply get along by going along.

A person of character, in short, will try to choose what is true and good and right in all decisions, small and great, that affect work, career, family and social life, the rearing of children, relationships with others, even leisure time.

Jackie Robinson knew that he was a human being made in the image of God. He recognized that innate dignity he possessed that St. Paul described so splendidly in Galatians today. All of us possess that same innate dignity. That dignity made Robinson strive to become a man of character, and so too should that dignity make us strive to become men and women of moral character. Paul's letter today tells us why.

THIRTEENTH SUNDAY
IN ORDINARY TIME

L ast week, I met a couple married fifty-some years. I asked, "What's the secret to such a marriage?" The wife answered, "Each week, we go to a restaurant for a delicious meal, fine wine, a little dancing, and then a slow walk back home." She added, "He goes on Tuesdays. I go Fridays."

Which reminds me, while out sipping wine with a friend, I noticed whenever he put the glass to his mouth, he would close his eyes. I finally asked, "Why do you do that?" He replied that the last time he had a medical checkup, the doctor told him never to look at a drink again.

The word of God takes us back in our imaginations to the ninth century before Jesus (the 800s), to two great prophets: Elijah and Elisha. God calls Elisha to succeed Elijah as a prophetic voice in a symbolic gesture. Elijah places his mantle, a symbol of power and authority, over Elisha. Elisha answered God's call with a "yes." He didn't know how his life would unfold; he simply trusted in God's design for him (1 Kgs 19:16b, 19–21).

God calls us to live a life of discipleship with Jesus. Not yesterday, today! What is our response to that call?

In his book *Through Seasons of the Heart*, John Powell, S.J., noted there is an old Christian tradition that God sends each person into this world with a special message to deliver, with a special song to sing for others, with a special act of love to bestow.

None of us is too young, too weak, or too old to deliver a message, sing a song, or bestow an act of love. Regardless of who we are, we have a mission to fulfill in this world. It was given to us by God himself.

This wisdom may be asking, are we answering God's call? As our life unfolds with its challenges and opportunities, do we trust in God? Paul, in his letter to the Christian community in Galatia, proclaims that Jesus has freed us from our worse selves (the vices of our dark side) so that we are free to live our better selves (a life of virtue). Yes, the Spirit of God lives and moves and breathes within us so that we can become our authentic selves, true sons and daughters of God our Father and heirs to the kingdom of God (Gal 5:1, 13–18).

Paul may be asking, how we are using our freedom? To become our authentic selves by practicing virtue?

In the Gospel according to Luke, James and John are angry at the Samaritans for not welcoming Jesus. Jews generally considered Samaritans foreigners despite their common heritage. The disciples want to obliterate these Samaritans for their lack of hospitality. But Jesus rebukes the disciples and continues straight to Jerusalem. On his way, someone asks to follow Jesus. Jesus answers, "Discipleship is making God your first priority" (Lk 9:51–62).

One theme in Paul's letter particularly intrigued me. Jesus has freed us so that we are free to become our authentic selves. And that's what joy and happiness is all about. Happiness is what everybody wants. But what's the secret to happiness? One author wrote that to be happy is the ability to do the following: forgive and apologize (we all make mistakes) and move on; listen to advice; keep your temper; share the blame; make the best out of the situation (most things in life seldom work out perfectly); and put the needs of others before your own desires. That's the secret to happiness.

Many think that if they get enough money, fame, or power, they'll be happy. But if so, explain how Elvis Presley, Marilyn Monroe, Prince, and other celebrities who "had it all" sedated themselves with drugs.

Happiness has to factor in the inevitable of life: work with its stresses; relationships with their tensions; disappointments with their dreams;

guilt about what one did or didn't do; health or the lack thereof; and ultimately death.

Bishop Robert Barron, of "Word on Fire" fame, likes to use Michael Jordan as an example of someone who became his happiest not by playing basketball any way he wanted but by mastering the basics.

So too with us. Mastering the basics of discipleship with Jesus. That's how we become our authentic selves.

St. Augustine reminds us that we, by our very nature, are oriented to God. The one thing we all need is a loving, ongoing relationship. But no human relationship will satisfy us completely, because we were created to live in relationship with God forever.

That is why Saint Augustine could write in his *Confessions*, his fourth-century autobiography, "O Lord, you have made us for yourself, and therefore our hearts are restless until they rest in You." No substitute for God will ever satisfy us.

So, what are the basics?

First, at one point in his ministry, many disciples left Jesus. Jesus then turned to his inner circle and asked, "Do you also want to leave?" Peter replied, "Master, to whom shall we go? You have the words of eternal life."

Yes, we become our happiest by mastering the basics (e.g., the beatitudes). Then we will become our authentic selves.

What sort of people should we be? In the opening verses of the Sermon on the Mount, Jesus answers the question. He describes the kind of character we should have. The first four steps focus on our relationship with God. The next four steps, our relationships with one another.

Disciples recognize they are empty and only God can fill their emptiness. That's what it means to be poor in spirit. Disciples are fragile creatures whom an awesome Creator gifted with life.

God didn't have to create us. Disciples realize their fortune to be alive and are grateful to God for that life, and they owe this awesome God praise and glory and honor.

Disciples beg for healing and salvation and know only God can comfort and heal them. They are meek and gentle, considerate and unassuming. Disciples, above all, hunger for a right relationship with God.

The next four beatitudes or attitudes or steps have to do with our relationships with one another.

Fortunate are they who forgive wrongs done to them and let go of their anger and resentment. God will be merciful to them because they realize how much they themselves need God's mercy.

Fortunate are they who are pure in heart, who have integrity, openness, sincerity, and authenticity in their relationships with others, they will see God face to face. The twentieth-century literary critic H. L. Mencken described conscience as the "inner voice which warns us that someone may be looking." That quote is a good guide for transparency in our relationships.

Fortunate are they who don't stir up conflict but try to be at peace with themselves, with others, and with God.

And lastly, fortunate are they who are ready to suffer rather than betray their conscience, who try to do the right thing in all decisions, small and great, that affect work, career, family, relationships, life.

I pray that these eight beatitudes will inspire us, disciples of the Master, to become our authentic selves, to live in a right relationship with God and one another forever.

FOURTEENTH SUNDAY
IN ORDINARY TIME

D uring Fourth of July weekend, we celebrate the Declaration of Independence that set in motion the great experiment we call the United States of America. No American document has had a greater impact on the wider world. In the human quest for freedom, equality, dignity, opportunity, and the rule of law, this document stands as a watershed. That's why we should pray this Fourth of July: God bless America so that we may increasingly become, and truly be, and long remain one nation, under God, indivisible, with liberty and justice for all.

In July, many of us think we need a vacation. At least I do. But I read something that warned whether I should take even one day off. Listen carefully, especially mathematicians.

We have 365 days in the year (right), but we take weekends off, subtract 104 days. That leaves 261 working days.

Our normal work day is eight hours a day. We do something else sixteen hours a day. So multiply that and subtract another 174 days.

That leaves eighty-seven working days. But wait! The average person consumes forty-five days per year at lunch. That leaves forty-two days. Plus breaks, figure twenty-one days per year. That leaves twenty-one days per year to actually work.

However, from those twenty-one days, subtract a two-week vacation. That leaves only eleven actual full workdays in the entire year.

Many companies also allow holidays. Subtract ten holidays from the eleven days: we've got one full workday per year.

This math may or may not be right, but I'm going to take some days off, and I hope you do too.

The word of God takes us back in our imaginations to the sixth century before Jesus, the 500s. It was a catastrophic time for ancient Israel. Babylonia destroyed the three pillars of Hebrew life: the king was dethroned, the temple was in ashes, and Jerusalem was a pile of rubble. Babylonia also deported many Hebrews to what we know today as Iraq.

Yet in the aftermath of this disaster, the author of third Isaiah speaks about a bright future. Jerusalem, like a mother nursing her children, will prosper and flourish again. A miracle (Is 66:10–14)!

Centuries later in Jerusalem, Jesus inaugurated new purpose in life through his horrendous death and glorious resurrection—another miracle!

Yes, our citizenship is in heaven. The author of Isaiah may be asking whether our lifestyle and behavior reflect this citizenship.

Paul, in his letter to the Christian community in Galatia (central Turkey today), proclaims that the death of Jesus on the cross / his resurrection from the tomb is our salvation. That's why Gentile Christians don't have to observe Jewish practices. Paul argued that God through the life-giving waters of baptism has transformed us into "new creatures," living temples of God, alive with the breath or life of God in us.

Paul goes on to say that the power of God has enabled him to endure all kinds of hardships for the sake of the Gospel (daily crosses, so to speak) and that same power of God enables us to practice a life of virtue—for example, self-discipline, honesty, responsibility, integrity, courage, friendship, compassion, and faith in God (Gal 6:14–18).

In the Gospel according to Luke, chapter 10, Jesus sends out seventy-two disciples to continue his saving and healing work. They are to travel light and trust always in God. And they reported back how they witnessed to the power of God.

Now what does it mean to witness? I'm a witness not simply if I see or say that something is true but if I actually experience it. I testify to something I myself experienced. For example, I ate veal marsala. I heard Beethoven's Fifth Symphony. I kissed the Blarney Stone.

The disciples were witnesses to Jesus in that sense. They walked with Jesus, talked with him, ate with him, and prayed with him. Peter reached out for his hand when he began to sink into the Sea of Galilee. Doubting Thomas put his finger into Jesus's side in the Jerusalem upper room. They saw him after he rose from the dead, watched as he was lifted up into the heavenly realms. And so Peter could preach, "This Jesus God raised up, and of that we are all witnesses."

We too are called to be witnesses to Jesus, like the disciples.

Every Sunday, in the creed, we testify to our core Christian beliefs: the triune God, the incarnation, the death/resurrection of Jesus, the dependable Spirit, the global community of disciples, life eternal. But what men and women look for in us, expect from us, is some visible sign that we have experienced what we believe.

Mahatma Gandhi put it well when he observed, based on his experience, "I like your Christ ... (but) your Christians are so unlike your Christ."

We will evangelize effectively only if we are a sort of sacrament, a symbol, an outward sign of God's grace/presence in us. We must not simply know about God; we must know/experience God. The heroes and heroines of Catholic Christianity knew/experienced God in their lives: Augustine, Francis and Clare of Assisi, Thomas Aquinas, Teresa of Avila, Therese of Lisieux, Mother Teresa, and many more.

We will touch people only if we have experienced God's grace/presence in us.

God gifts us with faith in Jesus Christ so that they can be witnesses to Jesus. We are by nature believers. Think about ordinary things we do. We turn on the car and expect it to start. We sit in the church pew; we expect it will support us. We turn on the house lights, and voila, there's light. We live by faith.

Our Catholic faith is a gift from God that empowers us to have a right relationship with the triune God as creator, redeemer, and sanctifier.

Faith is richer and deeper than belief. Faith calls us to enter into a relationship with Jesus Christ, to follow him, our way to eternal life, our truth who sets us free from falsehoods, and our light who illuminates the darkness around us as we journey toward our heavenly home. Faith is about connectedness to Jesus Christ. It's about our relationship with God that we nurture, especially through prayer.

Belief, on the other hand, is a statement about the essential truths of our faith that we proclaim every Sunday (e.g., in the fourth-century Nicene Creed).

But from faith comes a confidence about life. Why? Because we trust in a God who is always near to us, closer to us than we are to ourselves.

This confidence comes from having a purpose in life, taking risks, holding on to our beliefs, and building up an arsenal of small successes— and some failures. Successes convince us that it is possible to succeed in the future. Our failures tell us it is possible to survive and go on. Both are absolutely necessary in developing that sense of assurance that, in the end, things are going to be okay. We call this divine providence.

All of us are in the hands of an all-good God. And with a positive can-do, faith-filled spirit, we can work through, yes triumph over, the challenges we face in life. Why? Because God is always near to us, closer to us than we are to ourselves.

FIFTEENTH SUNDAY IN ORDINARY TIME

I just read about someone's morning prayer. It goes like this: "Dear Lord, so far today, I've done all right. I haven't gossiped, haven't lost my temper, haven't been greedy, grumpy, nasty, selfish, or overindulgent. And I'm very thankful to you for that. But ... in a few minutes, Lord,

I'm probably going to need a lot more help because I'm going to get out of bed!"

The word of God takes us back in our imaginations to the so-called law of ancient Israel. The word "Deuteronomy" in Greek means "second law." Unlike American law (well over two million laws in the United States), the law of ancient Israel was quite simple, easily understood, and readily accessible. That law, the author writes, is found within ourselves, within our own hearts: love God and love your fellow human being with all your heart and all your soul. I would call this "conscience." We have an almost instinctive judgment about the goodness or badness of our behaviors and attitudes. The author may be challenging us today to let our conscience—an informed conscience—be our guide in our behaviors and attitudes (Dt 30:10–14).

The passage from the letter of Paul to the Christian community in Colossae (in western Turkey) is really a hymn about the divinity and activity of Jesus Christ. He is the visible image of the invisible God, the revelation of God. Everything God ever wanted to say or do for us he did and said in Jesus Christ, the Word made flesh. Christ is the exemplar, the model or blueprint for God's universe. The universe is made in and through Christ, the incarnate Word. God entered into the human condition through Jesus Christ, who through his death and resurrection by the power and energy of the Spirit reestablished the relationship of human beings to God (Col 1:15–20). The letter of Paul invites us to give thanks for the gift of relationship, to make our lives Christ-centered.

In the Gospel according to Luke, the author tells the famous story of the Good Samaritan. Now the Samaritan in those days was persona non grata among the Jews, someone you would never be seen with. And that was the shock value of this parable. Who's our neighbor? Jesus says everybody is our neighbor, even this Samaritan. Every man, woman, child, whatever their ethnic background, sexual orientation, or religious tradition, is our neighbor. Jesus says very simply and yet very powerfully that we love God to the extent that we love one another. And in this parable of the Good Samaritan, Jesus challenges us to make random acts of kindness part of our daily routine (Lk 10:25–37).

We all have Good Samaritan stories. I came across an unforgettable one, a *USA Today* report by Jack Kelley about war-ravaged East Africa:

"We were in Mogadishu, the capital of Somalia, during a famine. It was so bad we walked into one village and everybody was dead. We saw this little boy. You could tell he was terribly malnourished; his stomach was protruding enormously. And when a child is extremely malnourished, the hair turns a reddish color, and the skin becomes crinkled as though the child's one hundred years old."

He went on: "Our photographer had a grapefruit, which he gave to the boy. The boy was so weak he didn't have the strength to hold the grapefruit, so we cut it in half for him. The boy picked it up, looked at us as if to say thanks, and began to walk back towards his village … When he entered the village, there on the ground was a little boy … It turned out to be his younger brother. The older brother knelt down, bit off a piece of the grapefruit, and chewed it. Then he opened up his younger brother's mouth, put the grapefruit in, and worked his brother's jaw up and down. We learned that the older brother had been doing that for his younger brother for two weeks. A couple of days later the older brother unfortunately died of malnutrition, but the younger brother survived."

I doubt that any of us will have to be a Good Samaritan the way that older brother was. But the point of the parable of the Good Samaritan is quite simple. Love of God is not genuine unless it includes love for our fellow human beings. And that's everybody. Every human being, no matter how young or old, healthy or sick, poor or rich, black or white, is made in the image of God. And in our love for and kindness to others, we most resemble God, who is love itself, and in our acts of kindness, we participate in the very life of God, who is indeed love.

One more Good Samaritan story about a young man who rose at five o'clock every morning and then worked fourteen hours. After two years, he told his parents that he just couldn't continue this. And then the youngster wrote to a former teacher, who promptly answered his letter—and praised this youngster, assured him he was gifted, and offered him a job. That encouragement changed this young man's life. He went on to become one of England's best-known novelists, Herbert George Wells, who authored nearly eighty books.

Again the point is simple: a kind word, a helping hand, a caring letter, a thoughtful call, a compassionate prayer—these little gifts of ourselves can make a big difference to someone else.

Jesus connects our love of God to our love for our fellow human beings. The judgment scene of chapter 25 in the Gospel according to Matthew says loudly and clearly, "When I was hungry, when I was thirsty, you did something." The point of that judgment scene is this: we can't say we love God and yet neglect our fellow human beings.

I close with an oft-told story about Giacomo Puccini, who wrote such operas as *La Boheme*, *Madame Butterfly*, *Tosca*, and *Turandot*. Puccini discovered he had cancer while writing Turandot. He began a race against death to complete this opera. He confided in his friend, the conductor Arturo Toscanini, saying, who will finish? Eventually death won; Puccini died in 1924 before he finished the opera.

For the world premiere performance of *Turandot* at Teatro alla Scala in Milan, Toscanini paid respect to Puccini in his own way. He conducted magnificently all the way up to where the master, Puccini, had left off. And then Toscanini stopped and cried out, "Thus far the master wrote."

The opera was completed by others. Which reminds me of the hymn paraphrasing Paul's letter to the Christian community at Corinth: Christ has no hands but our hands to do His work today. He has no feet but our feet to lead human beings his way. He has no voice but our voice to tell us why he died. He has no help but our help to lead human beings to his side.

Sixteenth Sunday
in Ordinary Time

A father told his three children when he sent them to college, "I feel it's my responsibility to provide you with the best education I can afford, and you don't owe me anything for that. However, I do want you to appreciate my sacrifice. So as a token, I want each of you to put $1,000 into my coffin when I die."

The children went on to become a doctor, a financial planner, and an entrepreneur.

When their father died and they saw him in the coffin, the three remembered his wish. First, it was the doctor who put ten hundred-dollar bills into the coffin. Then came the financial planner, who also put $1,000 in the coffin. Finally, it was the heartbroken entrepreneur's turn. He reached into his jacket pocket, took out his checkbook, wrote a check for $3,000, put it into his father's coffin, and took the $2,000 in cash. Now that's what some would label entrepreneurship.

The word of God takes us back in our imaginations over thirty-five hundred years to an ancient Middle Eastern legend about hospitality. Abraham, a man of extraordinary faith in God, sees three traveling strangers coming out of the desert. And he treats them as if they were his own family. He washes their feet and serves them a first-class meal. Abraham and Sarah welcomed these strangers as though they were welcoming God into their lives. And for their hospitality, God blesses Abraham and Sarah with a son, named Isaac (Gn 18:1–10a).

This legend invites us to be hospitable to those who enter into our lives. As a footnote, the Russian painter Rublev, in a famous icon, interpreted symbolically these three mysterious strangers as the Trinity.

Paul, in his letter to the Christian community at Colossae (western Turkey today), refers to the redemptive power of suffering (Col 1:24–28).

A modern-day author wrote that there are three inescapable parts of life: suffering, guilt, and death.

Suffering, from a Christian point of view, is ultimately a mystery. There's no satisfactory answer to this age-old inescapable reality. I think especially of the families of the eighty-four victims of the mindless violence in Nice, France. I think of Dallas. And Orlando. Surely the families of these victims must be asking, why?

Yet somehow we believe that inescapable suffering, accepted in faith, can be redemptive.

Why? Because Jesus, through his suffering, death, and resurrection, reestablished for us a right relationship with God.

Paul, who suffered much, invites us to ask God for the grace to unite our own inescapable sufferings to the redemptive sufferings of Jesus in whom we have eternal life. Why? So that our own suffering, like that of Jesus, can be redemptive for ourselves and others.

In the Gospel according to Luke, we have the story of Martha and Mary (Lk 10:38–42).

How many are sympathetic to Martha? My mother could be described as a Martha: a good chef, always busy preparing meals. And an aunt of mine could be described as a Mary: sitting comfortably, sipping her brandy Alexander. But in this Gospel, Martha and Mary can symbolize the two dimensions within each one of us: doing and talking; serving and praying. We have to be a combination of both: listening to the word of God in prayer, on the one hand, and doing good for others, for praying and serving go together.

Often, we fret or worry. We're busy shopping, chauffeuring, doing chores, working long hours. We often forget the one thing necessary: our relationship with God. Do we have our priorities straight?

Some of you may have read Rick Warren's popular book *The Purpose-Driven Life*. Life isn't simply a matter of acquiring and spending. Our ultimate purpose is to live in relationship with God and one another—yes, eternal life. The Martha in us challenges us to actively reach out to one another with our gifts and talents and treasure. Become involved, for example, in some volunteer service in the community. And the Mary dimension in us challenges us to pray.

The stomach rumbles for food, the mind itches for answers, and the spirit or soul hungers for God. The soul is the self: who I am.

There are many different ways in which to pray, to bring to consciousness the presence of God in our lives: familiar prayers like the Our Father or the Rosary, prayers of praise like the Psalms, slowly meditating on a biblical text, petitioning God for a favor, sitting quietly and feeling God's presence within us (through, for example, a mantra), actively participating in Sunday liturgies.

Almost anything can be a pathway into the awesome presence of God. But there is one common denominator: prayer lifts our minds and hearts up to God. Prayer is our longing for God and God's longing for us. Mother Teresa of Calcutta put it simply yet profoundly: "If we really want to pray we must first learn to listen, for in the silence of the heart God speaks … This speaking and listening is something that happens deep down in my heart: God speaks—I listen; I speak—God listens." Prayer is all about our personal relationship or friendship with God.

Begin every day then by spending at least ten to fifteen minutes in prayer, in the presence of God. People find ways to tune into God's presence as they go about their daily routine. Yes, take time to slow down so that you can tune into the presence of God. And on the weekend, gather with our faith community to celebrate the liturgy or mass.

So why don't we pray more often? One obstacle is our addiction to distractions. We are probably tuning into the TVs, computers, smartphones, noise, noise everywhere. People create so much noise that they can no longer hear the voice of God in their lives. That was the point of C.S. Lewis's *Screwtape Letters*. Finding time to pray simply depends on the importance we attach to connecting with God. One thing I find helpful in prayer is a focus—a candle, a crucifix, a religious image—something tangible to bring me back to God when I'm distracted by a call to be made, a chore to be done.

Another obstacle is the question: what's in it for me? What's in prayer for us is that prayer will make us better human beings—better spouses, parents, professionals, neighbors, better everything.

Someone compared prayer to the daily discipline of a musical performer. If I miss practice one day, I am the only person who may notice. But I notice. If I miss practice for a week and then perform, only a handful of people will be able to tell. But if I miss practice for two weeks, or three weeks, almost everyone can tell. If we neglect prayer for two or three weeks, almost everyone around us will recognize that we are not at our best.

I love St. Teresa of Avila's famous prayer:

Let nothing disturb you;
Let nothing frighten you;
All things are passing.
God never changes.
Patience obtains all things.
Nothing is wanting to them who possess God.
God alone suffices.

The word of God invites us to reflect on doing and talking, praying, and serving. Spending at least fifteen minutes a day in the presence of God is a good start for deepening our relationship with God, who will sustain us throughout our lives.

SEVENTEENTH SUNDAY
IN ORDINARY TIME

I just read a story about Pat and Mary, married in Ireland over sixty years. Pat, hospitalized multiple times, was told by the doctor that there was nothing more to be done. It was a matter of only days, the doctor said. Mary took Pat home, tucked him into bed, kissed him, and went down into the kitchen. Soon an aroma came wafting up the stairs. Pat cried, "Mary, what's that smell?" He struggled out of bed and slowly walked downstairs. On the kitchen counter were giant oatmeal raisin cookies. "Ah," Pat said, "my lovely Mary has made my favorite cookie for me before I die." He was just about to take a big bite, when Mary hollered, "Don't take even one bite. Those cookies are for the funeral." Talk about misreading the signs!

The word of God takes us back in our imaginations over thirty-five hundred years. Abraham is talking/praying with God about the fate of Sodom and Gomorrah. These two cities symbolize corruption, cities grossly inhospitable and perverse. Abraham engages in a spirited conversation with God about God's justice: why should the innocent suffer with the wicked? Abraham almost appears brazen, but that indicates the closeness of his relationship with God (Gn 18:20–32).

We know the end of these two cities. Some scholars say they were destroyed in a catastrophe of some kind, probably an earthquake. This story challenges us to ask ourselves, do we have a relationship with God? How do we pray? As a close friend? As a distant relative? Or as a stranger?

Paul, in his letter to the Christian community at Colossae (a city in western Turkey), speaks about the new identity we have through the waters of baptism. We have become sons and daughters of God our Father, heirs to the kingdom of God, graced by God to live a life worthy of our calling. God, through the death/resurrection of Jesus by the power of the Spirit, forgives us unconditionally so that we can live in relationship with God (Col 2:12–14).

Paul may be asking whether we live a life worthy of our calling.

In the Gospel according to Luke, the disciples want to know how Jesus talks to his heavenly Father. Jesus talks to God like a son or daughter with a parent, like a close friend with another close friend. Jesus urges us to be persistent in prayer, to go on asking, seeking, knocking, even though our heavenly Father already knows what we need (Lk 11:1–13).

There's a pattern to prayer that Jesus taught us in the Our Father. Here's a paraphrase. We pray thoughtfully:

> Our Father, because we are sons and daughters of God, family, heirs to the kingdom of God;
> Your name be honored and reverenced everywhere;
> May your kingdom of truth and justice and peace and freedom permeate everyone;
> And may your will be done on earth as it is in heaven.
> Satisfy our basic needs: food, health, home, a respectable livelihood, a good peaceful society.
> Forgive us for the things we do wrong as we forgive those who wrong us.
> And protect us from evils that will jeopardize our relationship with God.
>
> This is the pattern of prayer Jesus gave us.

The word of God today in Genesis and Luke invites us to reflect upon prayer, and the word in Paul's letter invites us to reflect upon God's unconditional forgiveness so that we can live in relationship with God forever.

When I think of modern examples of forgiveness, I recall Nelson

Mandela, who spent nineteen years as a political prisoner on Robben Island, off Cape Town, South Africa. He was forced to work in a quarry at least six hours a day, ate little, and lived and slept in a six by five cell. That he overcame hardship, that he saw the glory of God not only in his fellow prisoners but also in his jailers, was remarkable.

When Mandela was released from prison in 1990, he asked all Africans—black and white and colored—to seek not vengeance for injustices done through apartheid but to seek reconciliation and forgiveness from one another. That he was able to do this after years of hardship and cruelty and injustice was even more remarkable.

Mandela said he wanted to be remembered as an ordinary mortal (with all the peccadillos that go with being mortal) but with qualities that are within reach of ordinary people, like you and me. If Jesus could forgive, why shouldn't he. And if we can't forgive on our own, God simply asks us to participate in God's gift of forgiveness. Nelson Mandela recognized the possibilities for greatness within human beings, for forgiveness and peacemaking.

We are all sinners, Pope Francis reminds us. The third chapter from the book of Genesis, the so-called fall from grace, is really a sketch about how we sin: ingratitude, self-absorption/narcissism, the arrogance that believes that we can get along without God. "Sin" is one of the most basic terms in religious vocabulary, as common as "grace" and "God." Sin means being "out of sync" in our relationships with God and our fellow humans, missing the mark in the pursuit of our authentic self.

It's interesting to note that the only people who really upset Jesus were not sinners but hypocrites, those who refused to see anything wrong with their own prejudices, those who had no sense of a need for repentance, those who were smug about who they were.

But Jesus offered forgiveness aplenty to those who admitted they needed it. Amazing things are possible if we allow the Master to lay his forgiving hands upon us, an image captured powerfully in a poem by Myra Welch. Poems can be prayers. Here are some of my favorite lines from that poem about an old, battered violin whose tune changes:

> And many a person with life out of tune
> And battered and scarred with sin

Is auctioned cheap to the thoughtless crowd,
Much like the old violin ...
But the Master comes, and the foolish crowd
Never can quite understand
The worth of the soul and the change that's wrought
By the touch of the Master's hand.

May the touch of the Master's forgiving hand change us, and may the touch of our forgiving hands change our fellow human beings.

Eighteenth Sunday
in Ordinary time

You may have heard about three clergymen vacationing on the New Jersey Shore. One volunteered a confession: he has a problem with alcohol and finds AA meetings helpful. The second confided that he too had a weakness. He's coping with gambling and thanks God for Gamblers Anonymous meetings. The third clergyman admitted that he is a compulsive gossiper and can't wait to tell his friends what he heard. The moral of the story: be careful to whom you tell secrets.

The word of God takes us back to the wisdom literature of ancient Israel, the book of Ecclesiastes (aka the book of Qoheleth in the Hebrew Bible). Qoheleth probably is a preacher or "arguer" who reflects upon the transitory nature of life and the obsession of so many people with wealth—the possession of so many "toys." These, Qoheleth says, are empty pursuits. They won't make us happy. Ultimately, we will die and leave these so-called toys to someone else (Eccl 1:2; 2:21–23).

This invites us to reassess our own lives, to live a simple lifestyle so that others can simply live, and to be generous with what we have.

Paul, in his letter to the Christian community in Colossae (western Turkey), proclaims we are one with Jesus, new creatures by virtue of the waters of baptism. Therefore, focus on heavenly things. Practice virtue. Rid ourselves of vice, Paul says. Why? Because we are images of God, and our everyday behavior ought to reflect that likeness. Paul urges us to manifest the glory of God in our everyday attitudes and behaviors (Col 3:1–5, 9–11).

Jesus, in today's Gospel parable, calls the one who accumulates wealth only for him/herself a fool; they let greed trump generosity. The rich man tries to create a secure future. He forgets his absolute dependency upon God, his own mortality. Greed drives him to accumulate wealth. But for what? He dies that night. And someone else benefits from his greed (Lk 12:13–21).

I read about a woman named Henrietta Green who played the stock market so well that she accumulated $100 million at her death in 1916, about $2 billion in today's market. But unlike many of her wealthy contemporaries, Henrietta gave nothing to charitable causes and spent little on herself, her family, or her friends. She was what we would call a miser. She missed many opportunities to make a difference for the better in the lives of people. She simply used her money to make more money. And she died more infamous as the world's greatest miser than as the world's richest woman. She didn't have her priorities straight, like the man in today's Gospel parable. Plenty wasn't enough, and once he died, he had nothing. As the saying goes, "You can't take it with you."

Yes, we have to have things we need to live, but the only things we can take with us in death are our good deeds. I never saw a truck with money following a hearse. And so Jesus urges us to make sure we have our priorities straight. Seek first the kingdom of God.

Did you ever wonder what really happens after death? Over eight million people in America say they have had near-death experiences. Some describe hearing themselves being declared dead, being lifted out of their bodily selves and seeing a figure blazing with light reaching out to them. Then they come to a boundary. Finally, they feel themselves being pulled back into their bodily selves. Some would argue that these are self-induced or hallucinatory visions.

But one thing is certain: either we go on or we don't. There's no middle ground.

Blaise Pascal, a French mathematician and philosopher, faced this dilemma. Confronted with two irreducible options—one of which had to be true, one of which had to be false, one appealing, one alarming—and having no certain way of knowing which was true, the only realistic option was to go with the appealing choice.

In other words, when the doorway to death opens, I believe "I'm entering into a new, indescribably transformative, happy life." And if I'm wrong, Friedrich Nietzsche won't be thumbing his nose at me, saying, "I told you so." I simply won't be. And neither will Nietzsche.

The reality of death challenges us to answer the most important questions in life: how shall we live and what shall we do? It's interesting to note that the Roman Senate decreed that each time a victorious general entered triumphantly into Rome with his booty and slaves, someone stood behind him, holding a golden wreath over his head and whispering into his ear, "Memento, mori! Remember, you will die."

The so-called last things—hell, purgatory, and heaven—are challenging beliefs in Christianity. How can we say at the same time there's an all-good God and there's a hell?

If you would like to imagine the last things, I suggest you begin with Dante's *The Divine Comedy*. Dante imaginatively reveals how he awoke in a dark wood (perhaps a midlife crisis) where Virgil leads him through earth to hell (remember Dante's famous line, "Abandon hope, all ye who enter here"). They see sinners undergoing punishments in nine descending circles until they reach a frozen lake, the abode of Satan. Then they emerge to begin their ascent to the seven cornices of purgatory, and finally, with his beloved Beatrice, Dante climbs the nine heavenly spheres of paradise and into the dazzling vision of the Trinity.

The Divine Comedy is a masterpiece in poetry, not easily readable but profoundly instructive about life, especially hell, purgatory, and heaven.

Heaven and hell answer the question of justice. Many good people die without receiving in this life an adequate reward for their goodness, and many wicked people die without paying for their wickedness. If there's such a thing as justice, there has to be some place where wrongs are righted, good rewarded.

So what are hell, purgatory, and heaven? The language is best understood symbolically rather than literally. God does not "send" us to hell; we freely choose to go. Also, although we must accept the possibility of hell (in light of the dynamic between divine love and human freedom), we don't have to believe that human beings are actually "in" such a "place." In fact, we hope all human beings will find salvation.

But if we peel away its fiery imagery, hell can be described simply as the absence of God. It is the ultimate failure to realize our true selves, whereas heaven is the ultimate fulfillment of our true selves. In heaven, we participate in the mystery of God. Purgatory then is a "purification" in which we become our true selves. And judgment is our own recognition of what is true and false in ourselves.

Finally, we believe that in the mystery of death, God will transform our earthly selves, like Jesus, into a new, indescribable heavenly reality. St. Paul put it well when he wrote, "No eye has seen, no mind has ever imagined … what God has prepared for those who love Him." May today's word of God challenge us to get our priorities straight and seek first the kingdom of God.

Nineteenth Sunday

in Ordinary Time

How many saw the opening ceremonies of the Olympics in Rio de Janeiro? A media extravaganza for a TV audience of umpteen million: music; dance; marches; flags from 206 countries; nearly 11,000 athletes, including 553 from the United States. The Olympics highlight not only the dreams for medals in thirty-six events; they also celebrate the values of peace, understanding, self-discipline, and excellence, values that people of goodwill everywhere strive for in their relationships with fellow human beings.

We celebrate the Olympics for many good reasons. They excite and inspire. We treasure moments when an athlete does the seemingly impossible, or when the truly gifted makes the impossible seem routine. We're thrilled when a person or a team overcomes great odds. And we are touched by genuine camaraderie among teammates and between competing teams.

I have one story about teamwork. You may have heard about a police officer who pulled over a couple for speeding. The husband sheepishly told the officer, "I had the car on cruise control at sixty." The wife chimed in, "Sweetheart; you know the car doesn't have cruise control." The husband turned to his wife and said, "Would you please let me handle this?"

The wife answered, "You should be glad your radar detector beeped." As the officer thought about a second ticket for the illegal radar detector, the husband barked, "Please let me do the talking." Then the officer noted, "I see you're not wearing your seat belt. That's also a fine." The husband explained, "I had it on but took it off when you pulled me over so I could get my license." The wife interjected, "Sweetheart, you never wear your seat belt."

As the officer pondered a third ticket, the husband yelled at his wife, "Please let me handle this!" The officer then asked the wife, "Does your husband always shout at you?" And she answered, "Only when he's drinking."

The moral of the story: there's a time to speak and a time to refrain from speaking.

The word of God today takes us back to the wisdom literature of ancient Israel—generally pithy pieces of advice about how to live and behave.

Think about some of the common-sense wisdom of your grandparents/parents.

"A penny saved is a penny earned." Government should heed that advice. A national debt in the trillions?

Or "a stitch in time saves nine." If a station master in Italy spotted that two trains were going in opposite directions on the same track, toward each other, twenty-five passengers could have been saved.

"Haste makes waste." If our nation weighed strategically the pros and cons of its involvement in foreign affairs, perhaps we wouldn't have so many messes.

The wisdom in the Bible is as good advice today as it was centuries ago.

The author of the book of Wisdom remembers the extraordinary first Passover meal, when the Hebrews celebrated their Exodus or liberation from their oppressors in ancient Egypt. The author then continues: that same provident God, always faithful to his promises, eventually will send the promised Messiah who will usher in a kingdom of peace and justice and truth and freedom (Wis 18:6–9).

The author of this book counted his blessings, and so too should we.

The letter to the Hebrews tells of two faith-filled people, Abraham and Sarah. I am amazed at the risks they took when Abraham heard the call of God, trusting completely in God as he traveled to a land he didn't know, through deserts and villages full of strangers, staying in shelters, and believing that Sarah would at last have a child. Abraham and Sarah are models of faith, trusting always in an all-good God, despite the uncertainties they faced (Heb 11:1–2, 8–19).

We might ask whether we strive to be models of faith in our families and communities.

In the Gospel according to Luke, Jesus says that we are to be like servants who await their master's return from a wedding, ready to welcome him when he comes and knocks. The author quotes Jesus: be alert; be prepared; focus on what truly matters—eternal life with God. We will be accountable for the kind of person we become with the time and talent God gives us (Lk 12:32–48).

I like to imagine that God entrusts to each one of us a mass of stone, or a lump of clay if you will, to sculpt a disciple with the time and talents we have. To be a disciple of Jesus is to be fundamentally a man or woman of faith, someone who trusts completely in God throughout all the opportunities and challenges and disappointments of life, someone who desires to do what God wants even though we can't always precisely figure out what that is. It's the desire that's important.

The letter to the Hebrews particularly invites us to reflect upon the dimensions of our own faith. Faith is, first and foremost, a gift from God whereby we begin a relationship with the triune God, a relationship that we nurture especially through prayer. It is the acceptance of God's promises as true and a commitment to live accordingly. Faith also includes the essential truths we profess every Sunday in our Nicene Creed, from the fourth century.

Faith, in other words, is living in a relationship with God. And just as there can be various stages in our moral development (Lawrence Kohlberg, for example, proposed six stages), so too there can be various stages in our faith development (James Fowler proposed six stages).

We either grow into a relationship with God, or we fall out of that relationship.

This faith compels us to share our faith with others. A college professor once challenged students to share their faith with someone else. The images that sprang to the students' minds then were clergy in pulpits, revival tents, Joel Osteen on TV, Jehovah Witnesses ringing doorbells. And these students weren't going to ring doorbells.

Many of us share our faith with others even though we may not realize it. Parents/grandparents share their faith whenever they teach their children/grandchildren the virtue of prayer, generosity, fairness, honesty, and service to others. So do teachers when they do their best to develop those virtues or habits of heart and skills of mind that will enable students to become good citizens. So do medical professionals when they calm fearful patients with a word of encouragement, and so do citizens share their faith when they urge their elected officials to vote for legislation that will promote human dignity and the common good. We especially share our faith when we do our best to stand up for what is right and true and good.

The only Gospel some people may ever see or read is ourselves. The word of God in Hebrews invites us to be men or women of faith like Abraham and Sarah. How? By doing the best we can each day. Don't live a life of regrets. Every day, we have so many little opportunities to do good for others. As the Nike saying goes, just do it.

TWENTIETH SUNDAY

IN ORDINARY TIME

I read about a fellow walking along a Florida beach. He came across an oil lamp in the sand. He picked up the lamp and gave it a rub. A genie appeared and told him he would be granted one wish. The man thought for a moment and said, "I want to live forever." "I'm sorry," said the genie, "I'm not allowed to give eternal life." "Okay. Then I want to die after Congress balances the budget and eliminates the debt." "You shrewd fellow," said the genie. "That will take an eternity!"

The word of God takes us takes us back to the sixth century before Jesus (the 500s), to a national crisis. The army of Babylonia has surrounded Jerusalem. The Hebrew king is uncertain. Should he continue fighting and die, or should he surrender and survive?

Jeremiah advises surrender in light of Babylonia's overwhelming military superiority. But the king's advisers, who want to fight a losing battle, call Jeremiah a traitor and have him thrown into an empty cistern to die. The king, of course, foolishly continues battling Babylonia and loses. Eventually, the king orders Jeremiah to be rescued from the well (Jer 38:4–6, 8–10).

Jeremiah's mission was to call the Hebrews to fidelity to God's covenant. More often than not, they chose infidelity, and so Jeremiah predicted the collapse of Jerusalem. Jeremiah may be asking us, how faithful are we to our baptismal promises? Do we live a God-centered life?

The author of the letter to the Hebrews speaks about witnesses to the faith who should inspire the early Christians to persevere, to fix their eyes on Jesus (Heb 12:1–4). We too have our witnesses in such splendid heroes and heroines as Francis and Clare of Assisi, Ignatius of Loyola, Teresa of Avila, Vincent de Paul, Therese of Lisieux, Saint Teresa of Kolkata. These and many more are witnesses to the faith worth studying in our own quest for meaning, in our own search for God. They cheer us on.

In the Gospel according to Luke, Jesus speaks not about peace but about conflict. Jesus preached a message that was clearly divisive. He challenged what was false and demonic. You're either with him or against him (Lk 12:49–53).

Just as Jesus experienced conflict, so too should we expect conflict in our lives. Every one of us faces conflict or confrontation of one kind or another. Such confrontations are not only inevitable, they can make for better human relationships, an opportunity to clear the air, to set a relationship back on a healthy course.

Some people try to avoid conflict at all costs, thinking that nice people don't get angry. But conflicts can lead to constructive solutions and stronger relationships.

Some of you may recognize the classic film/Broadway play *A Raisin in the Sun*. The basic story line is this: A family suddenly inherits $10,000. What to do with it? The mother wants a small house for the family. The daughter wants to realize her dream of going to medical school. But the son persuades the mother to let him start a business with a friend. Then the so-called friend skips town with the money. The family is suddenly in the midst of conflict.

The point is simple enough: sometimes people disappoint us, sometimes they make messes out of their lives and the lives of those closest to them. But in a situation with multiple challenges, the mother in the play had it exactly right: there's always something left to love. And the worse things are, the more there is to love. The family in the play emerged stronger.

We have to lift up, forgive, support, and love especially those who may disappoint us. To paraphrase the twentieth-century British author Rudyard Kipling in his poem "If," which I highly recommend for its profoundly practical advice, "If you can keep your head when all are losing theirs."

Here are some guidelines for arguing fairly, so that conflicts can be a healing rather than a hurting, a constructive rather than a destructive experience.

1. When we have a bone to pick with someone, we need to set up a time to settle the issue as soon as possible. Why? We don't want to bottle up our anger indefinitely. Setting an agreeable time and place allows us to cool off and sort out the real issue.

2. Clarify carefully the particular behavior we object to. For example, leaving dirty clothes on the floor makes more work for me. Always make "I" statements rather than "you" statements. "I" statements avoid name-calling ("you're" inconsiderate), generalizations ("you" never think of anyone else), abusive language ("listen, airhead"). Avoid these negative judgmental words; always distinguish the behavior we find objectionable from the negative judgments about that behavior. For example, someone is late. A negative judgment would be: you never think about anyone but yourself. The actual behavior is: you're late; maybe there was a highway accident. Address the behavior and avoid negative judgments that inevitably undermine a relationship. All relationships call for nurturing if they are to become stronger.

3. Express your feelings honestly. A wife whose husband was always late for dinner without calling showed her annoyance one night by leaving him a plate of dog food. She obviously was expressing her feelings through her actions, and fortunately her husband was good humored about it. Disguising our feelings, however, instead of expressing them, can be dangerous, like using the silent treatment. Feelings are neither positive nor negative; they are facts. Just as aches and pain in our bodies alert us to physical problems, negative feelings alert us to problems in our relationships. There's nothing wrong with expressing feelings honestly and calmly.

4. Lastly, come up with creative solutions. The goal of any conflict is to resolve a problem in a way that is agreeable to both parties. We may have a specific request that will resolve the issue (like telling a teenager to play the drums some time other than midnight). Many times, though, we cannot think of a solution. Then we brainstorm. The more ideas, the better. Sometimes, we may come up with a new creative solution to the problem; sometimes we may decide to live with an unsolvable problem. We simply agree to disagree.

There are many other guidelines for arguing fairly. For example, actively listening to what the other person is saying, not taking ourselves too seriously, staying calm, spelling out agreements, and so forth. Many of these we know, but in the heat of an argument, we can easily forget.

St. Paul wrote centuries ago, "Love does not brood over injuries." All of us must be willing to forgive, forget, and be friends. If we have fun together and communicate regularly, then we create a climate of love, respect, and trust in which our relationship will not self-destruct under the strain of occasional conflicts.

When all else fails, turn to chapter 6 of Luke: Be compassionate as your heavenly Father is compassionate. Do not judge, and you will not be judged; do not condemn, and you will not be condemned. Pardon and you will be pardoned.

Twenty-First Sunday
in Ordinary Time

I read about someone who didn't like the headstone at her husband's grave. So she gave her daughter $3,000 to buy "a lovely stone." A year after she died, one of her sons stopped at the gravesite before he went to his sister's home for a holiday dinner. He saw the same old stone at the grave. So he asked his sister, "Didn't Mom ask you to buy a new stone?" The sister replied, "Yes. I'm wearing it on my finger. Isn't it a lovely stone?" So much for miscommunication!

The word of God takes us back to the sixth century before Jesus. In a vision, the author sees all people, Jews as well as non-Jews, going up to Jerusalem into the temple, the symbol of the glory or presence of God, to worship the one true God (Is 66:18–21). The author invites us to recognize the image of God in all people and to worship the one true God, Creator of us all.

The author of the letter to the Hebrews alludes to the age-old philosophical question, why do bad things happen to good people? Of course, there's no satisfactory answer to human suffering and natural disasters (e.g., floods, fires, earthquakes) (Heb 12:5–7, 11–13).

The author proposes that hardships can help us realize our true selves as sons and daughters of God our Father. Inescapable suffering especially, accepted with trust in an all-good God and joined to the sufferings of Jesus, can be saving and healing for ourselves and others.

Why do I say that? The sufferings of Jesus were precisely that—saving and healing for all.

In the Gospel, Jesus continues "on his way" (a code in Luke for his passion and death), and the disciples ask, "Will only a few people be saved?" Jesus indicates that many who think themselves respectable or high and mighty will not be included in the kingdom of God, and many who are considered disreputable and down and out will be (Lk 13:22–30).

God's ways are not our ways. Salvation is ultimately a gift from God, not something we earn. Jesus says that we have to struggle to enter through that symbolic "narrow gate" into the kingdom of God. To quote the Gospel according to John, Jesus is indeed the gate to eternal life, our way, our truth, and our life.

Many people struggle through so-called narrow gates as they go through the cycle of human development from adolescence to old age.

I think of the movie *Brooklyn*, a charming story. Eilis Lacey grew up in a small Irish village in the 1950s. There aren't many opportunities for her there. With the encouragement of her sister Rose, Eilis decides to open the door to a new life in Brooklyn.

She doesn't have a promising start: she's seasick on the ocean crossing; letters from home exacerbate her homesickness; and she feels lost in the fast-moving pace of New York City.

But people along the way help Eilis walk through the narrow gates she encounters in Brooklyn: a priest, the landlady, the department store supervisor. She gradually sees a future, a new life, beyond the door she opened.

Suddenly Eilis is called back to Ireland for a family emergency. She reenters that door she closed and confronts her guilt for leaving. Then, on her way back to America, Eilis befriends another young woman like herself. Eilis notes, "You'll feel so homesick that you'll want to die, but you will endure it and it won't kill you. And one day the sun will come out. And you'll realize … this is where your life is."

Many times, we can only go through so-called narrow gates or doors of life by letting go of our fears and doubts, by realizing that God is with us as we open these doors into an uncertain future. Our faith in particular can sustain us as we pass through, because it helps us overcome these fears and doubts, because it satisfies our basic needs. How is that?

Our faith fosters a healthy self-image. We are made in the image and likeness of God, and through baptism, we become living temples of God. God lives within us, and we live within God. He is closer to us than we are to ourselves. And people with a positive, healthy self-image generally engage in constructive behavior.

Second, our faith satisfies our longing for happiness. We are forever seeking the transcendent, something beyond ourselves that will give purpose to our lives. St. Augustine wrote, "O God, you have made us for yourself and our hearts are restless until they rest in you." Within every human, being there is a subconscious quest for the ultimate, the all-good. We call this God. Our primary purpose in life is to live in relationship with God and one another. In the hereafter of heaven, we will see God face-to-face with all our yearnings for happiness satisfied.

Third, our faith gives us a sense of belonging. We are a community of believers who go back two thousand years, with heroes and heroines who inspire us as we go through the narrow gates of life in the cycle of human development, saints who encourage us in our pursuit of God and God's pursuit of us. We are linked together by a common bond of faith, grace, and baptism. We gather regularly to offer God gratitude and worship for our lives, to acknowledge our absolute dependency upon God our Creator and to ask God in the Our Father prayer to satisfy our basic needs for food, health, home, a respectable livelihood, and a good, peaceful society. These encounters with the triune God are wrapped up in the mystery of the sacraments.

We are a community not only of heroes and heroines but also of sinners and scoundrels. Not everyone is as good as we would like. Some are dysfunctional. We have to live with some messiness and muddle through as best we can. But when we fail, when we sin and jeopardize our relationship with God and one another, Jesus assures us that God's mercy outweighs our failures. We struggle each day. God gave us the sacraments of initiation, healing and service, grace and power to help us through the narrow gates of our lives.

Finally, our Catholic faith provides us with a guide in the Bible, with the best news ever: how God offers each one of us salvation through Jesus. The Bible contains poetry, prayers, songs, genealogies, history, prophecies, stories, exhortations, and teachings that demonstrate God's unconditional love and forgiveness and acceptance of us. The risen Christ is present in these scriptures proclaimed in our liturgies. God speaks to us, and we listen; we speak to God, and he listens.

As we go through the many narrow gates or doors of life with its fears and doubts in the cycle of our human development, our Catholic faith will sustain us so that we can eventually enter safely through that final gate into the kingdom of God.

Twenty-Second Sunday
in Ordinary Time

I read a story about a man and a woman involved in a car accident. Both cars were demolished. After they crawled out of their cars, the woman said, "Wow, our cars are totally demolished, but we're okay! This must be a sign from God that we should be friends." Flattered, the man replied, "Yes, I agree. But you're still at fault … you caused this accident."

The woman continued, "And look—another miracle. This bottle of wine didn't break. Surely God wants us to drink this wine and celebrate our good fortune." She handed him the bottle. The man drank half the bottle and then handed it back to the woman. The woman took the bottle, put the cap back on, and handed it back to the man. The man asked, "Aren't you having any?" The woman replied, "No. I'll just wait for the police." That's what I call one-upmanship.

The word of God takes us back to the wisdom literature of ancient Israel, the book of Sirach. Here the author, Ben Sira, asks us to be always humble, to recognize who we really are: creatures dependent upon an all-good Creator (Sir 3:17–18, 20, 28–29).

We each appear on this planet at one particular moment at birth, and disappear at another particular moment in death. William Shakespeare, whose four hundredth anniversary of death we recently celebrated, captured the transitory nature of life when Macbeth reflected, "Life's but a walking shadow, a poor player that struts and frets his hour upon the stage and then is heard no more."

The biblical author challenges us to remember that no matter how famous or powerful or wealthy we are, we are what we are by the grace or favor of God. Hence, do all the good you can. By all the means you can. In all the ways you can. In all the places you can. At all the times you can. To all the people you can. As long as ever you can.

That's the only thing—the good we do—that we will take with us in death.

The letter to the Hebrews contrasts two assemblies, one in Egypt where God made a covenant with the Hebrews in the midst of thunder and lightning, and the other assembly in the heavenly Jerusalem where countless creatures, angelic as well as human, celebrate the new covenant or relationship God made with us through the bloody death and glorious resurrection of Jesus. Yes, God has bestowed his favor, his grace upon us in the waters of baptism and has transformed us into his sons and daughters, coheirs to the kingdom of God (Heb 12:18–19, 22–24).

The author challenges us to live a life worthy of that calling.

In the Gospel, Jesus is again sitting at a table. He already had a reputation for ignoring the dinner rules of Miss Manners. After seeing how the so-called rich and famous proudly took the places of honor, Jesus told a parable in which he compares the kingdom of God to a celestial banquet; Jesus is the host, and all are welcome. But who will be seated? The humble, the people we least expect to see there (Lk 14:1, 7–14). The twentieth-century Catholic author Flannery O'Connor captures this scene powerfully in her short story "Revelation." The biblical author may be asking whether we will be humble enough to recognize who we really are, creatures absolutely dependent upon an all-good Creator God, and thus have a place at the heavenly banquet.

What is humility? Humility doesn't mean being a doormat or cipher. Nor should it be associated with lack of self-esteem. The word "humility" derives from the Latin word *humus*, "ground" or "soil," and can be understood simply as down-to-earth, knowing who we are, where we came from, and where we're going. Humility is grasping the truth about ourselves as creatures with limitations and shortcomings. The humble Mary, Mother of God, showed what humility is in her Magnificat: "My soul proclaims the greatness of the Lord ... the Mighty One has done great things for me" (Lk 1:46–55).

Yes, Mary rejoiced in the gifts or favors God bestowed upon her, but she, a creature, recognized that God, her Creator, was the giver of every favor she had. So too should we, creatures, rejoice in the gifts God, our Creator, has given us.

Pride is the opposite of humility. It thinks we are self-sufficient, as if there's no God, as if we are accountable to no one except ourselves.

The book of Genesis gives us an insight into humility. Chapters 1 through 11 can be understood as a parable that teaches a profound truth. We are made in the image and likeness of God. That is our dignity. But then in Genesis, we overstepped our limits and preferred to play God instead. We wanted to be number one. And what happened? Death— the breaking and collapse of all of our relationships on all levels. Adam and Eve hid from God, they argued and blamed each other, and the land produced sustenance only with toil and sweat. They sinned. Sin or wrongdoing can be understood as being alienated from relationships or missing the mark in these relations. With sin, our relationships broke down. To break off our relationship with God, the source of life, is to cut off our air supply, so to speak, to die.

Hence, we are born into a broken world. That is the Catholic understanding of original sin, a phrase St. Augustine coined. We are like Adam and Eve, and the other characters in these primal Genesis stories, they mirror us, trying to play God in chapter 3, inciting violence, perpetuating injustices, forgetting God and building monuments to ourselves like the Tower of Babel. If you don't think there's something out of kilter on this planet, look at the daily news.

Chapters 1 through 11 in Genesis are really a story about ourselves and the damage we do when we play God. That is pride. Humility is the opposite—recognizing that we are simply creatures with limitations and shortcomings, absolutely dependent upon an all-good God. Luckily for us, God had the final word, and that's why God became one of us in Jesus of Nazareth who, through his horrible death and glorious resurrection, reestablished these broken relationships.

The Christian answer to the questions "Who are we? What is the ultimate purpose of our lives?" acknowledges the tensions that are at the very core of our being. We do what we know we shouldn't do, or don't do what we know we should do. Our lives are indeed transitory—the Bible repeatedly emphasizes this theme—and yet we possess dignity, the life of God. God dwells in us, and we dwell in God.

The Christian intellectual tradition emphatically says that there is no human solution to the brokenness on our planet. But it goes on to say there is a power beyond us (God) that can heal this brokenness. And this awesome, all-good, and transcendent power became flesh in Jesus of Nazareth and is alive in our midst by the power of the Spirit. This same God invites us to live a life of discipleship with Jesus, to be attentive to others in ordinary ways, to be generous with what we have, so that one day we can sit down at the banquet table of eternal life.

Twenty-Third Sunday
in Ordinary Time

L abor Day, a national holiday since 1894, is an invitation to take pride in our work and to recommit ourselves to doing the best we can.

There's an ancient wisdom tradition that says God sends each person into this life with a special message to deliver, with a special song to sing for others, with a special act of love to bestow.

No matter who we are, no matter what we do, all of us, from a Christian perspective, have a mission to fulfill. God has committed some work to each one of us that he hasn't committed to another.

And so whatever your life's work is, do it well! As one author put it, if it falls to your lot to be a street sweeper, sweep streets like Michelangelo painted frescos on the ceiling of the Sistine Chapel, like Shakespeare wrote poetry, like Beethoven composed music; sweep streets so well that all the hosts of heaven and earth will have to pause and say, "Here lived a great street sweeper who did his/her job well." And isn't that what holiness is all about? Doing our life's work as best we can.

You may have heard about the political candidate, trailing in the polls and speeding down a street to speak at a huge rally; he was late and desperate for a parking spot. Looking up to heaven, he pleaded, "Please, God, find me a parking space. And if you do, I will always stand up for what's right in the legislature, go to church regularly, become a role model," and on and on. Suddenly a parking place appeared. The candidate looked up again and said, "Never mind, God. I found a space." So much for politics.

The word of God takes us back to the wisdom literature of ancient Israel. The author asks, who can understand the "things of the earth" or even the "things in heaven"? The author highlights the transitory nature of human life with all its limitations and shortcomings. But, says the author, take courage; God gifts us with wisdom to discern what's right (Wis 9:13–18b).

Fyodor Dostoyevsky proposed in his classic *Brothers Karamazov* that "if God does not exist, everything is permissible." Some may wonder whether today's so-called gurus and pundits are trying to marginalize God in the public square. The author challenges us to anchor our lives in the wisdom of God and the things of God, to do the right and love goodness and walk humbly with God.

St. Paul, in a letter he wrote from prison, asks his friend Philemon, a Christian slaveholder in Colossae, Turkey, to welcome back a runaway slave whom Paul loved as a brother in Christ. Philemon could have had the runaway executed, so Paul pleads that he forgive this slave and love him as a brother because we are all brothers and sisters of Jesus Christ, sons and daughters of God our Father (Phlm 9–10, 12–17).

Critics may ask, why didn't Paul condemn slavery? Some, of course, will excuse Paul by arguing that the society and times were different. But that begs the question. In any case, Paul sees the dignity of every human being and asks us, do we see one another as brothers and sisters of Jesus Christ?

In the Gospel according to Luke, Jesus challenges us to make discipleship our first priority. In the two parables here, Jesus cautions us not to naively rush into discipleship without gauging the cost (Lk 14:25–33).

Discipleship is our first priority. Yes, God will bestow upon us the grace, the power and energy of the Spirit, to persevere in a life of discipleship with Jesus, who is our way, our truth, and our life. In times of darkness, Jesus is our light; in times of brokenness, Jesus is our healer; and in times of depression, Jesus is our counselor.

Yes, we pray that we will persevere. Perseverance generally means working steadily to achieve the good things we set out to do. We obviously can't do everything. But if we commit ourselves to worthy goals, like discipleship, we can achieve many good things.

There are many examples of perseverance, religious as well as secular. I give you two: Mother Teresa of Calcutta and the Wright brothers.

Pope Francis declared Mother Teresa of Calcutta a saint before tens of thousands of international visitors in St. Peter's Square and millions more watching on international news. She is a model of perseverance in faithfulness to God, prayer, and love.

Born to a devout Catholic Albanian family in present-day Macedonia, she traveled to Ireland to join the Sisters of Loreto. In 1929, she embarked for India, where she entered the Loreto novitiate and then began teaching.

Seventeen years later, en route to a retreat, Teresa felt the calling to work among the poorest of the poor. Eventually she left the Sisters of Loreto, studied the basics in nursing, and began to care for the poor, sick, and dying on the streets of Calcutta.

In 1950, she founded the Missionaries of Charity, whose numbers expanded exponentially to over three thousand sisters today. There is also a male branch of the congregation and an association of Lay Missionaries of Charity. The missionaries continue to minister to the sick and dying in some of the poorest areas in the world. They have touched the hearts of millions of people of all faiths.

Mother Teresa showed us holiness. Through a life of prayer despite her own "inner spiritual darkness," and through a desire to meet people's basic need for love, she taught us the priority of prayer and service in realizing one's true self as a son or daughter of God our Father. She found purpose, led, and gave her best.

The following poem by an unknown author expresses for me that spirit:

> Fortunate are the persons who in this life can find
> A purpose that can fill their days and goals to fill their mind.
> For in this world there is a need for those who'll lead the rest,
> To rise above the "average' life by giving of their best!

Will you be one, who dares to try, when challenged by
the task,
To rise to heights you've never seen, or is that too much
to ask?

Another example of perseverance is the work of Orville and Wilbur Wright, whose airplane innovation dramatically changed the way we travel. Back in their day, journalists, armed forces specialists, even friends and family laughed at the idea of an airplane. They scoffed, "Leave flying to the birds." But the Wright brothers persisted. And a place called Kitty Hawk, North Carolina, became the setting for the launch of an airplane. The rest is history.

There are hundreds of examples of perseverance. But, in light of the Gospel theme, may God grace us with the energy and power of the Spirit to persevere in our life of discipleship with Jesus, like Mother Teresa, so that we can indeed be coheirs to the kingdom of God.

Twenty-Fourth Sunday
in Ordinary Time

I just read a story about effective communications. Getting your message across is critical.

Consider the mother who hollers to her son, "You get down here this very minute because you're late for school." The son hollers back, "I don't want to go to school. The kids don't like me. The teachers don't like me. And everyone is talking behind my back."

The mother rushes upstairs and points to her son and says, "You get out of bed this very minute, because you are going to school for two reasons: You're forty years old. And you're the principal."

That's effective communication.

The word of God carries us back in our imaginations to the thirteenth century before Jesus (the 1200s) to the charismatic Moses. On Mount Sinai, Moses is conversing with God like a friend, praying, and at the base of the mount, the Hebrews, just liberated from their oppressors in ancient Egypt, are breaking the covenant they had just renewed with God by worshiping a replica of the gods of Egypt (Ex 32:7–11, 13–14).

We do the same sometimes, don't we? We create idols—for example, money, power, celebrity status—and make them our be-all and end-all at the expense of everything else, even eternal life. We forget who we are—creatures absolutely dependent upon an all-good Creator.

But Moses here does some straight talking. He intercedes for the Hebrews in prayer and asks God to forgive them for their wrongdoings. And God does. The author challenges us not only to ask God for forgiveness but also the grace to live a life worthy of our calling.

Paul, in his letter to Timothy, confesses: yes, he fiercely persecuted Christians; he was the worst of sinners. And yet God in a mystical encounter with Paul in Syria turned Paul's life upside down and graced him to become one of the greatest evangelizers in Christianity.

And then Paul cries out that prayer: "To the king of ages, incorruptible, invisible, the only God, to God alone honor and glory forever and ever" (1 Tm 1:12–17).

Paul gratefully challenges us to be grateful to God for our blessings.

In the Gospel according to Luke, Jesus tells three parables. God is likened to a shepherd who searches hills and crevices until he retrieves the lost sheep. God is likened to a woman scouring the house until she finds the lost coin. And God is likened to a father whose son runs away and returns home flat broke, to be embraced by a loving father who throws a party (Lk 15:1–32).

In all three parables, God never gives up on us. Like the "hound of heaven" in Francis Thompson's poem, God relentlessly pursues us until he catches up with us. The words of that poem are riveting:

I fled him (i.e., God) down the night and down the days.
But with unhurrying chase, and unperturbed pace,
Deliberate speed, the feet beat—and a Voice beat ...
I am He (God) whom Thou seekest.

The point is God never gives up on us even though we may give up on God. God loves us unconditionally, forgives us unconditionally, and accepts us unconditionally.

I would like to explore forgiveness in light of the parable of the prodigal son. Here are two true stories—one about the lack of forgiveness, the other about forgiveness.

Simon Weisenthal raised the question, how does one forgive the unforgivable? Many in his family died in Nazi concentration camps. In his book *The Sunflower,* Weisenthal tells how one day a nurse came to where he was working, tapped him on the shoulder, and told him to follow her. He was taken to a young SS trooper who was dying.

The soldier told Weisenthal how his SS unit rounded up the Jews in a particular zone, herded them into a building, doused it with gasoline, and shot those who tried to escape. This horrible atrocity haunted the young soldier, who wanted forgiveness. He begged Weisenthal for forgiveness. Weisenthal simply got up and left without saying a word.

Later on, this troubled Weisenthal. Should he have forgiven the dying young soldier? The Nazis had murdered his own family, had committed horrible atrocities. Weisenthal concludes with a question: "what would you have done if you were in my shoes?"

Now put yourself in the soldier's shoes. What if others are unable to forgive us? And what about the people we've wounded and who won't forgive us, who can't forgive? We want forgiveness so badly, as that young soldier did.

It is then that Jesus steps into the shoes of the Simon Weisenthals and comes to our broken hearts and says, "All is forgiven." When people can't forgive, or won't forgive, Jesus will.

The Gospel challenges us to forgive. And if we want forgiveness, and the people we have wounded can't or won't, then we will discover that Jesus Christ will stand in their place. This is also why Jesus gave us the sacrament of penance or reconciliation. It's the place where we are reconciled to God. It's the place where Jesus says, "I, on behalf of all those you have wounded—brothers, sisters, parents, children, relatives, friends—all those people who will not forgive, I will forgive." The parable leaves us with two questions. "Am I someone who won't forgive? Before I die, I'd better come to terms with this parable. Or am I the young soldier who may have forgotten to ask Jesus for forgiveness when others won't forgive? Before I die, I'd better beg Jesus for forgiveness."

That's a true story about lack of forgiveness; here's one about forgiveness.

In 1983, during the Christmas season, two men sat in a prison cell in Rome. One was in a blue sweater and jeans, the other in a white cassock and skullcap. *Time* magazine described the photo: in an extraordinary moment of grace, the violence in St. Peter's Square was transformed. In a bare, white-wall cell, John Paul II tenderly held the hand that had held the gun that was meant to kill him.

For twenty-one minutes, the pope sat with his would-be assassin,

Mehmet Ali Agca. The two talked; once or twice, Agca laughed. The pope forgave him. That photo challenges us to forgive.

There's a folk wisdom that says "forgive and forget." But sometimes we can't forgive wrongs done to us unless we remember—for example, a once-happy relationship, then a wrong done, and finally, a shattered relationship. At times, we have to forgive ourselves as well as others so that we can move forward with life. Sometimes, to forgive as Christ forgives is impossible to do on our own.

But Christ doesn't ask us to forgive on our own. He simply asks that we participate in his gift of forgiveness. God has already forgiven those who are truly sorry, and all he asks us to do is to participate in his forgiveness. Forgiveness is possible when we trust in God to bring healing and forgiveness and reconciliation to our broken relationships.

As God constantly searches out the lost, so should we, and as God always welcomes back the estranged, so should we.

Twenty-Fifth Sunday
in Ordinary Time

A friend told me Pope Francis urged priests in his exhortation *Evangelii Gaudium* (*The Joy of the Gospel*) not to give long homilies. The briefer, the more effective. My friend went on to say, "Remember, the Ten Commandments are only 297 words; the Bill of Rights, 463 words; Lincoln's Gettysburg address, a mere 266 words. Obamacare regulations, on the other hand, 11,588,500 words." Rest assured, my homily will follow Pope Francis's advice.

The prophet Amos today alludes to the lack of sensitivity and compassion in our relationships.

I share a story about a schoolteacher, Jean Thompson, and a fifth-grade student called Teddy. He didn't seem to pay attention, wore messy clothes, and, unknown to her, had a learning disability. As their first semester progressed, Jean's assessments of Teddy became less positive.

When the Christmas holidays came, the students brought little gifts to the teacher's desk—all in brightly colored paper, except for Teddy's. His was wrapped in brown paper with crayon scribbled on it. She opened it, and out fell a bracelet with most of the stones missing, and an almost empty bottle of ordinary perfume. The youngsters giggled. Jean put some of the perfume on her wrist, put on the bracelet, held her wrist up, and said, "Doesn't it smell lovely? Isn't the bracelet pretty?"

At the end of the day, when the children left, Teddy said, "Miss Thompson, all day long you smelled just like my mother. And her bracelet, that's her bracelet, it looks nice on you, and I'm really happy you like my presents." When Teddy left, she cried.

Jean's attitude changed. She tutored Teddy and helped him catch up. Time passed, and Jean lost track of Teddy. Seven years later, she got this note: "Dear Miss Thompson, I'm graduating from high school, and I'm second in my class. I wanted you to be the first to know. Love, Teddy."

Four years later, a note: "Dear Miss Thompson, college has not been easy, but I'm graduating." Another four years later: "Dear Miss Thompson, as of today, I am Dr. Theodore J. Stollard. How about that? I'm going to be married in July. And I want you to come and sit where my mother would have sat, because you're the only family I have. Dad died last year." Jean sat where his mother would have.

Jean was a decent and loving human being who reached out to one student when he needed help most, and she set him on a career path where he could do much good for others.

There are millions of Teddys, children who are left out and left back, who will never become professionals or much else, partly because no one with a heart made a difference. This was a story at the elementary-school level, but at all levels of human development, we need to be reminded that similar miracles can happen, if we have the heart to make a difference.

The prophet Amos, eighth century BC, challenges us to deal with people compassionately.

Amos here spoke up against rigging prices, inflating currency, and cheating consumers. Too few were getting richer and richer, he declared, and too many were getting poorer and poorer. Amos targets those especially who are so greedy that they will even rig their scales to cheat the poor (Am 8:4–7).

Amos might be asking whether we treat one another fairly, as we would like to be treated.

The letter to Timothy urges us to pray for our political leaders so that ordinary people may live tranquil lives. Pray especially that our political leaders will possess the true wisdom to choose what's right for the common good of our country and our global community. Paul goes on to proclaim that Jesus is our one mediator who reconciles all human beings to God and through whom all have eternal life (1 Tm 2:1–8).

Paul might ask us, do we pray to God for our political leaders, that God will grace them to choose with integrity what's right?

In the Gospel according to Luke, Jesus tells a parable (a story with a message) about a manager who's about to be fired. So what does this parable have to do with the kingdom of God? The manager, at a critical moment, when his entire future was at stake, acted decisively to deal with the crisis and planned shrewdly to secure his future (Lk 16:1–13).

In fact, Jesus creates a crisis in our lives when he preaches the kingdom. We have to act decisively, plan shrewdly to ensure our place in God's kingdom.

Today I would like to follow up on an overriding theme in the book of Amos—our relationships.

Jesus connects our love of God to our love for one another. Matthew 25 says this loudly and clearly: "When I was hungry, when I was thirsty, you did something." The point of that judgment scene is this: we can't say we love God and yet neglect our fellow human beings.

Our love for one another doesn't depend upon what they can do for us. After all, who were the beneficiaries of Jesus's love? By and large, they were people who couldn't do much in return.

Jesus makes some radical demands upon us with regard to our relationships with one another. Read carefully chapter 5 in Matthew. For example, Jesus says, "Give to everyone who asks." It's not always possible. But that particular demand indicates the thrust or direction of our lives: we have to be generous with what we have, especially with our time, talent, and resources.

Jesus says elsewhere, "To the person who strikes you on one side of the face, offer the other side as well." Sometimes we do have to stand up against wrongs; we may even have to take someone's life in self-defense. Again, Jesus indicates the thrust or direction of our lives—that is, we should do our best to be peacemakers, healers, bridge builders, reconcilers, forgivers.

Now these radical demands of Jesus of course have to be linked to the mission of Jesus. Jesus proclaims that the kingdom of God is here but not completely or fully here. You and I are living in between the historical coming of Jesus in Bethlehem and the final coming of Jesus in glory and power at the end-time.

So we live in the tension between the ideal and the real. And often we fall short of the ethical ideals of Jesus because we have within ourselves a so-called pull or tendency to not always choose the good. We call this tendency original sin.

But the grace or power of God within us can overcome this tendency within ourselves and strengthen our relationship with God and with one another. How? By being generous. And by being peacemakers within and outside the family.

All of us have the potential to do great things for God. And it begins with small, ordinary things. Think back to that teacher and youngster.

So, I pray that the word of God will inspire us to nurture our relationships with God in prayer and serve our fellow human beings compassionately and generously.

Twenty-Sixth Sunday
in Ordinary Time

I read about a Father O'Malley in Ireland who looked out the window one day and noticed a donkey lying dead on the lawn. He promptly called the local police. The conversation went like this. "Good morning. This is Sergeant Smith. How might I help you?" "The best of the day to you, Sergeant. This is Father O'Malley at St. Mary's. There's a donkey lying dead on my front lawn, and would you be so kind as to send some lads over to take care of the matter?"

Sergeant Smith thought he would have a little fun, and replied, "Well now, Father, it was always my impression that you took care of the last rites." O'Malley replied deftly, "Yes, it's true, but we are obliged to notify next of kin first, which is the reason for the call." Moral of the story: don't mess with an Irish pastor.

Anyway, I begin with a pertinent story a fellow friar told me. A man complained to a psychiatrist friend that despite his great wealth, he felt miserable. The psychiatrist took the man to the office window overlooking the street and asked, "What do you see?" The man replied, "I see a woman, some children, and an elderly couple." The psychiatrist then took the man to stand in front of a mirror and asked, "Now what do you see." The man said, "I see myself."

The psychiatrist then explained, "When you look through the glass of the window, you see other people. But when you look into the glass of my mirror, you see only yourself. The reason for this," said the psychiatrist, "is that behind the glass in my mirror is a layer of silver. When silver is added, you cease to see others. You see only yourself." It's amazing the difference silver can make. The silver in the mirror, or the silver of money, changes everything.

The point is whatever we have—money or talent or time—all comes from God. And when we lack generosity and become absorbed in gaining more and giving less, we become like the characters in Amos and Luke today.

Today's Gospel parable describes two contrasting lifestyles. One of the characters is the man who has everything. He lives splendidly like a king. But outside the gatehouse, at a distance, is a poor man who has nothing. Even in death they differ. The rich man probably is buried with pomp and circumstance. Poor Lazarus is likely left unburied. But then there's a dramatic reversal of fortunes. Where do we find the rich man? In Hades or the so-called netherworld. A tormented man! And where do we find poor Lazarus? In the embrace of Abraham. A happy man! A chasm separates the two (Lk 16:19–31).

Now why is the rich man condemned? Not because he's wealthy. He is condemned because he didn't see Lazarus. He neglected Lazarus. The rich man committed a sin of omission. He didn't listen to the prophets of ancient Israel—for example, Amos, in today's first reading (Am 6:1a, 4–7). The rich and famous of ancient Israel, Amos said, pampered themselves at the expense of others. Their conspicuous consumption was at the expense of those who lacked the basic necessities of life. They never heard the phrase *live simply so that others can simply live.*

The rich man forgot the prophets who said, "This is what the Lord requires of you: only to do the right and to love, and to walk humbly with your God." Sometimes we too, like the rich man, don't listen to the prophets like Amos. Sometimes we don't even listen to what Paul in his letter to Timothy tells us to do: practice virtue so that we may have eternal life through Jesus Christ.

Someone wrote. "Twenty years from now, we will be more disappointed by the things we didn't do than by the ones we did." Live a life of no regrets. Don't regret something you could have done but didn't; after all, we only live once. As the saying goes, our everyday lives are not a dress rehearsal. To the extent that our lives are in our own hands, do good now. Don't regret not doing good, as the rich man later regretted not helping Lazarus.

Some of you may remember the actor John Barrymore, who electrified audiences with his portrayals of Hamlet and Richard III. Barrymore wrote that "a man [and a woman] is not old until regrets take the place of dreams."

Yes, quietly sit down somewhere in the next few days and write your own obituary. What do you want to be remembered for? Take stock of your life.

Now back to the rich man in today's Gospel. Let me tell you about someone who lived a life of no regrets, a woman who was generous to others with her time, talent, and family treasure, a model of generosity, a woman who exemplifies the power of action over words.

When Katherine Drexel was in her twenties, she was one of the wealthiest women of her time. Born in Philadelphia right before the Civil War, she was the daughter of a wealthy international banker; in fact, the family firm grew into the Wall Street powerhouse Drexel Burnham Lambert.

Katie Drexel experienced a turning point in her life when her family was vacationing in the west. She saw Native Americans mistreated and living in extreme poverty. She witnessed African Americans living in squalor. She saw them dehumanized by prejudice and racism. She became so passionate about helping Native and African Americans that she decided to do something. In 1889, at age thirty, this heiress to the Drexel fortune joined the Sisters of Mercy. Two years later, she founded her own community, the Sisters of the Blessed Sacrament.

Katherine Drexel used the income from her father's trust—$350,000 per year in the early 1900s (a lot of money then)—to build over one hundred schools in the rural west and south, including Xavier University in New Orleans, the first university in the nation for African Americans. She also fought for civil rights, taking on the Ku Klux Klan and funding some of the NAACP's investigations into the exploitation of blacks.

Unlike the rich man in today's Gospel, she put her money and her life where her heart was. Her life reflects an important lesson in the Gospel—the power of deeds over words. Jesus is quite clear: promises can never take the place of performance; words can never be a substitute for deeds. Christ demands that we as his disciples profess our faith not just in the prayers and rituals we utter but in the good we do and support, the positions and candidates we uphold, and the relationships we form.

Yes, the parable of the rich man and Lazarus is a wake-up call to you and me to live a life of no regrets. To do good today, not tomorrow. To use our time, talent, and treasure for the good of others now, not later. And so I pray that Katherine Drexel, like so many other heroes and heroines in Christianity, may inspire us to do good today, and I pray that today's parable will warn us: Jesus demands deeds, not words.

Twenty-Seventh Sunday
in Ordinary Time

E very now and then, I like to leaf through children's letters to
God. They give a different perspective. Here are a few I recently
discovered.

Dear God,
Did you really mean "do unto others as they do unto you"? Because if
you did, then I'm going to fix my brother.

Dear God,
Thank you for my baby brother, but what I prayed for was a puppy.

And finally for now,

Dear God,
Maybe Cain and Abel would not kill each other so much if they had
their own rooms. It works with my brother.

The word of God from the book of Habakkuk describes the sixth
century before Jesus (the 500s). Ancient Babylonia conquered Israel. The
prophet sees war, violence, and death everywhere. It sounds almost like
Syria today. The prophet cries out to God, "How long will you tolerate
all these evils?" And then God lets the prophet see more clearly a vision

of the future. God will keep the promises he made; good ultimately will triumph over evil, life over death. In the meantime, the prophet urges the Hebrews to stay the course, do what is right, to trust God even when they doubt God's presence (Hb 1:2–3; 2:2–4).

Paul in his letter challenges Timothy to do the same—to be courageous, not cowardly, to persevere and not waver. Why? Because God is always with us, even though at times God appears hidden. The Spirit of God empowers us to stay the course. The risen Christ anticipates what we one day hope to become: transformed into new heavenly creatures with God and one another forever. Paul urges you and me to stay the course (2 Tm 1:6–8, 13–14).

In the Gospel according to Luke, the disciples beg Jesus to bestow upon them the gift of faith so that they too can work signs and wonders for God. Jesus simply says, "You already have plenty of faith. Now practice that faith" (Lk 17:5–10).

Yes, we can work wonders for God by forgiving those who have wronged us, by being hospitable to those who may have lost their way in life.

In light of the prayer in the Gospel, let us pray, "Lord, increase our faith," so that we can be instruments or channels of God's blessings to one another.

I would like to speak about an extraordinary person of faith whose feast day we celebrate October 4: Francis of Assisi.

Who was Francis, the thirteenth-century founder of the worldwide Franciscan movement? He has been described variously as a lover of animals, an environmentalist, a peacemaker, a mystic, a reformer, a poet. But who was he really?

Francis came from a middle-class Italian family. Twice he went off to the wars in that region and failed miserably.

Then he had a dream that compelled him to go back to Assisi. There he began to wrestle with the fundamental questions of human life: Who am I? What am I living for? What is the ultimate purpose of my life? Francis yearned for something greater than himself that would give meaning to his life and answer these questions. In silence and in prayer, he began his own search for God. "Who are you, oh Lord, and who am I?" he asked.

Eventually, Francis gave up every "thing" he had; he experienced his own creaturehood, his own nothingness. And in that experience, he found everything—God, an all-good God; a God who became one of us in Jesus of Nazareth; a God who is alive in our midst by the power of the Spirit, especially in the sacramental life of the community we call the church. Francis began to pursue the Gospel in a literal fashion, and eventually men and women began to gather around him to form what we know today as the one million-plus Franciscan family.

Now we may wonder, does the thirteenth-century Francis have anything to say to us in the twenty-first century? I believe we can capture his message in three incidents.

One incident took place at La Verna, not far from Florence, Italy. Francis was praying, and suddenly he experienced the stigmata or marks of the crucified Jesus in his hands, feet, and side. This captures the depth of Francis's relationship with God; he had such a close friendship with God that God gifted him with the stigmata.

Francis challenges us to deepen our own relationship with God. We can do this in many ways, especially through prayer and liturgy. I would like to add the family dinner table. In our own words, thank God for the blessing of one another and for the food we have. And in our prayer, we may keep specific people in mind (e.g., a sick relative or friend). On special occasions (e.g., a birthday), you may want to light a candle to celebrate a milestone in one's life.

The table is also a good place to reaffirm forgiveness and to ask such questions as, am I generous with my things, my time? How well do I appreciate my family?

Another incident that captures the message of Francis occurred as he prayed before the crucifix in the tumbledown chapel of San Damiano. He heard the crucified Jesus tell him, "Francis, rebuild my house which you see is falling into ruins."

Francis at San Damiano challenges us to build up our family life. Jesus lived in a family. Holiness in families comes from learning to forgive and to ask for forgiveness, learning to face family problems and challenges, and doing something about them together.

Spending time together as a family is important. What we do together is not as important as that we do things together. Watching and discussing a video or TV program or playing a game together can be an enjoyable family experience. Welcoming into our homes the people we know and especially friends of our children is another way of strengthening family life. Other people can enrich our own perspective.

The third incident that captures the message of Francis was this: As he rode one day along a road, out stepped a man with leprosy. Francis started to ride away. But no! Francis slowly climbed down from his horse and embraced the leper.

Francis saw in that leper the brokenness of human life. A leper can be described as someone who lacks wholeness. In our own lives, we experience this, in ourselves and in other people.

Pope Francis, in his encyclical *Lumen Fidei*, wrote: "How many men and women of faith have found mediators of light in those who suffer! So it was with Saint Francis of Assisi and the leper, or with Mother Teresa of Calcutta and her poor."

This planet of ours, in some ways, hasn't changed much since the times of Francis. There are so many ways in which we can be healers, peacemakers of broken relationships. Francis was able to cut through the trivial questions of life and focus upon the essentials.

May the life of Francis inspire us to intensify our life of prayer with God, to build up one another with our time and talent, especially in family, and to reach out with a healing hand to those whose lives have been broken.

TWENTY-EIGHTH SUNDAY
IN ORDINARY TIME

C hristopher Columbus symbolizes, for me, perseverance. Probably born in the seaport city of Genoa, Italy, he was mesmerized by the sea and became a sailor and explorer. If the world was round, he surmised, you can reach the east by sailing west around the globe. But no one would finance the voyage.

Columbus didn't give up. Eventually, advisers to Ferdinand and Isabella of Spain convinced them to finance the exploration. The gamble paid off handsomely. Yes, Columbus was a derring-do sailor, a skilled navigator, a man of vision. But most of all, he symbolizes perseverance. He never gave up on his dream. And neither should we give up. Not all of our dreams will come true, but some will if we persevere.

The word of God takes us back in our imaginations to the ninth century before Jesus, to a man of God by the name of Elisha. And here a foreigner, a Syrian army general, begs the prophet to heal him, to cure his disease. To the surprise of the general, Elisha simply suggests that this foreigner bathe in the Jordan River. Eventually the Syrian does, is cured, and praises the God of Israel (2 Kgs 5:14–17).

This passage invites us to praise God for who he is, our Creator, and what he does, the many blessings he bestows upon us.

Paul, in his letter to Timothy, speaks about the hardships he has endured for the sake of the Gospel. Wherever he goes, he fearlessly preaches Christ, once crucified and now risen. Paul invites us to give thanks for the gift of God's life, bestowed upon us in the waters of baptism, nurtured in this liturgy, and ours forever in a transformed heavenly life (2 Tm 2:8–13).

In the Gospel according to Luke, Jesus heals ten lepers. Only one, a foreigner, returns to give thanks to God (Lk 17:11–19).

I flash back to a true story in our Franciscan soup kitchen in Philadelphia, St. Francis Inn. One cold and rainy night, an old woman with all her possessions in three shopping bags sat at a table, ate a sandwich and sipped soup, got up, and disappeared into the night.

When a friar was cleaning up, he picked up her bowl, and beneath the bowl were four pennies. She had left a tip. As little as she had, this old woman, a bag lady, was grateful for what was given to her. It's a powerful reminder to all of us to be grateful to God for our blessings.

Gratitude presupposes indebtedness. All of us are indebted to many people: to our parents, teachers, our best friend, our soulmate, and above all, to God.

Yet at times we feel shortchanged; someone else is wealthier, better looking, better talented, with a better set of genes, and with fewer problems. And we take many people for granted. We easily forget how lucky we are. Half the people in the world go to bed hungry, 70 percent can't read, 80 percent are in substandard housing, according to some statistics.

If our dinner tonight will be different from last night's, we're breathlessly blessed. But the essential question is whether we are breathlessly grateful.

The twentieth-century British author G.K. Chesterton wrote that people sometimes ask whom to thank for the presents in their stockings on Christmas morning. But they rarely think to thank someone for putting legs into the stockings they put on every day.

Gratitude segues into another word, "Eucharist," which means thanksgiving, not just for good health or prosperity but thanks to God for being born and for being called to be a son or daughter of God our Father, thanks for being invited into the life-transforming centerpiece of Catholic spirituality, the Mass, where bread and wine are transformed really and truly into the reality of the risen Christ.

This is indeed the wonder of wonders. Yet it seems so many have lost their sense of wonder. When a remarkable twentieth-century rabbi named Abraham Heschel awakened from a near fatal heart attack, he told a friend visiting him, "My first feeling was ... only gratitude to God for my life. I was ready to depart. 'Take me, O Lord, I have seen so many miracles in my lifetime.'" Heschel wrote in his book, *I Asked for Wonder*, "I did not ask for success; I asked for wonder, and you, O Lord gave it to me."

We can easily get distracted, even at Mass. Who's here. Who's not. Who's wearing what. Yes, there are so many things that can easily distract us from this wonder of wonders—the risen Christ sacramentally and mystically in our presence. We don't go to Mass to socialize or to be entertained. We go to give ourselves to God and in return to receive God.

Let me suggest that when we walk in, we might simply ask God, "In this Mass, show me one way I can become a better version of myself this week." Then listen. Listen in the quiet of your heart to what God is saying to you in the music, through the prayers, through the scripture readings, the homily. Is there one thing that strikes you? A word, a phrase! Then spend the Mass praying about how you can live that one thing in the coming week. "Show me, O Lord, how I can become a better version of myself this week."

Let's quickly rediscover the workings of the Mass. We begin with the introductory rites, especially the penitential rite. "What thoughts, words, and behaviors have not helped me become the best version of myself?" Identify a specific thought, word, or behavior that has become an obstacle between you and God and others, and ask for forgiveness.

Listen to the Liturgy of the Word. That word is the privileged expression of our faith. God is the author of that word in the sense that it contains what God want us to know about God, God's relationship with the universe, and God's purpose for us. The authors of the word were real authors. But God inspired them to write the truth about God and our relationship to God, and yet the way they expressed these truths and the languages, images, literary forms, and the worldview they used remained their own.

God speaks to us in the word, and we listen. We speak to God, and he listens. Is there a word or a phrase that God is whispering into our soul? What's the one thing that will help us become a better version of ourselves? Perhaps here, more than anywhere else, God wants to speak to us.

And then the liturgy of the Eucharist, the thanksgiving—the great Eucharistic Prayer with its Last Supper narrative and consecration and Communion—where the risen Christ truly presences himself to us in the signs of bread and wine, and where we become one with him in Communion and then are sent forth to continue the saving work of Jesus Christ.

The Mass reveals God's vision for us, God's dream for us to become the best version of ourselves.

Yes, the Mass is a profound mystery—God's blueprint for all creation. It is indeed the centerpiece of Catholic spirituality, God's unfathomable gift to us. Embrace that gift every week.

TWENTY-NINTH SUNDAY
IN ORDINARY TIME

A pastor was sitting in a local McDonald's eating lunch. As he opened a letter from his mother, a twenty-dollar bill fell out. He thought, *Thanks, Mom. I could use that.* But as he left, he noticed a person on the sidewalk leaning against a light post. He thought, *That fella could probably use twenty dollars more than I.*

So he put the twenty dollars back in the envelope and wrote "Persevere!" The man took it and smiled.

The next day, the pastor happened to be back at McDonald's eating. The same man handed him a big wad of money. Surprised, the pastor asked, "What's this?" The man replied, "It's your half of the winnings. Persevere won at the track, at thirty to one." That's an example of perseverance paying off handsomely.

The word of God takes us back to a defining moment in the life of ancient Israel: the Exodus or the deliverance of the Hebrews from their oppressors in ancient Egypt. In their wilderness wanderings toward the promised land, the Hebrews encountered dangers everywhere. Here they are probably fighting for land and water rights. Moses, atop a hill, displays the staff of God, symbol of God's presence, and extends his hands in prayer. Every time Moses lifts his hands up prayer, the tide turns in favor of the Hebrews (Ex 17:8–13).

The message is simple: persevere in prayer, despite all obstacles, because God does hear us even though he may not always answer us in the manner we would like.

Paul speaks to Timothy about the significance of the word of God. God breathes in the scriptures and inspires and empowers us, Paul writes, to stay the course, to live a life of discipleship with Jesus despite the challenges. Yes, the word of God is indeed a guide to our lives (2 Tm 3:14–4:2).

In the Gospel according to Luke, we have a story about a crotchety, heartless judge and a persistent widow. And because the widow doesn't give up in her demand for justice, the judge eventually caves in and gives the widow what is rightfully hers. The parable challenges us to persevere, to do what we can to right wrongs (Lk 18:1–8).

I would like to highlight the significance of the Bible, in light of Paul's letter to Timothy.

These days, there seems to be an intense interest in the occult. People play with Ouija boards, have their fortunes told, and read horoscopes. They forget that in the Bible we can meet the living God in our quest for nourishment in our spiritual life.

What is Catholic spirituality? It's simply living our lives in the presence of God. It is letting "the Breath or Spirit of God" live and breathe and work in us. And the fruits of that "Breath or Spirit of God" are "love joy, peace, patience, kindness, generosity, faithfulness, gentleness, self-control" (Gal 5:22–23).

There are many different spiritualities in Catholic Christianity: Benedictine, Franciscan, Dominican, Jesuit, Marian, and so on. All are different responses to the one common Christian call to holiness. The goal, to paraphrase the musical *Godspell*, is to "see Thee, O Lord, more clearly, love Thee more dearly and follow Thee more nearly, day by day." And we attempt to do this in our own unique circumstances.

Let me propose a biblical spirituality. Did you ever wonder whether God speaks to us? In fact, he does! God speaks to us through the inspired word of God, the Bible, a privileged form of conversation between God and us, a two-way conversation. That's why we should be ever attentive to the word of God, especially in the liturgy. God authored the Bible in the sense that the Bible includes what God wants us to know about God, the universe, and ourselves.

The human authors of the Bible employed the languages, images, literary genres, and worldviews they knew in their cultures to communicate religious truths, not scientific truths. The authors knew nothing about evolution, the solar system, galaxies, planets, and extraterrestrial life.

The Bible is not one book but a library of books written over 1,500 years by at least forty different authors—in prose and poetry, fiction and history, historical narratives and short stories, genealogies and sermons, parables and letters, songs and codes of law, blessings and curses, prophetic and proverbial sayings, and apocalyptic visions. Some books in the Bible evolved over decades; others over centuries. They are not always easily understandable.

Catholics recognize that the biblical writers used various forms of communication or literary forms. And just as we interpret literary genres differently today, so too we have to interpret biblical literary genres differently. The writers definitely were not communicating scientific truths. We say, for example, the sun rises/sets. Actually, the sun doesn't rise or set. So, we first must know what kind of genre the writers were using. Then we will be able to discover more easily the fundamental religious truth that it is trying to communicate. Moreover, the Bible often speaks symbolically, as in the parables of Jesus.

The two creation stories, for example, communicate religious truths: God is our awesome Creator; we are mere creatures; everything God created is good; man and woman are made in the image of God, but they broke their friendship with God and often choose their worse over their better selves. We call this fall from grace "original sin." But how did the biblical author communicate these religious truths? Through the cultural images and traditions they knew.

Finally, I invite you to read the Bible prayerfully. We read not to find specific answers to questions the biblical authors never thought about but to become the kind of person for our day that Jesus was for his day.

The scriptures in particular point to Jesus as the unique or definitive revelation of God to us. In other words, everything that God wanted to do for us or say to us, God did in Jesus. In this sense, there will be no new revelation. However, the Spirit in the global Catholic community guides us along the journey to our heavenly dwelling place, in light of new challenges in new generations and evolving cultures.

I invite you to nourish your spiritual life through the Sunday readings in the Liturgy of the Word. Think about it. In many ways, we are a Sunday people. We gather every Sunday in churches across the globe to give ourselves to God and receive God in return, to listen to God in the Liturgy of the Word and to presence the risen Christ sacramentally in the liturgy of the Eucharist, to become one with Him in Communion, and then are sent forth to continue the saving work of Jesus Christ.

God speaks to us in the word, and we listen; we speak to God, and he listens. Is there a word or a phrase that God is whispering into our souls? For me, that word today is perseverance. Last Sunday, it was gratitude. Perhaps here, more than anywhere else, God wants to speak to us.

May we listen to God speaking to us in the Sunday scriptures, and may that word transform us into the best version of ourselves so that we will indeed be channels of God's grace to one another.

THIRTIETH SUNDAY
IN ORDINARY TIME

P aul's letter to Timothy about his own readiness for death reminds me of a fellow who lived recklessly, and eventually, as he approached death, he wanted to put his life together to be ready to meet his maker, God.

The family called their pastor, who celebrated the rite of reconciliation for the man. The pastor asked, "Do you renounce Satan?" No reply. The pastor shouted into the dying man's ear, "Do you renounce Satan?" And the fellow slowly opened his eyes and said, "Look, I don't want to antagonize anyone at this time." Now that's what I call weighing all your options.

The word of God carries us back in our imaginations to the wisdom literature of ancient Israel, the book of Sirach, written probably in the second century before Jesus (Sir 35:12–14, 16–18).

This literature reads like a guide to ethics especially for people in public service. It's about the art of living well in the best sense of the phrase. Hard work, honesty, integrity, compassion, responsibility, courage, respect, self-discipline, and faith in God are the true measure of character. Perhaps our presidential candidates would benefit from a reread of this book.

Here the author says God has no favorites. But then he goes on to say that God definitely hears our prayers, especially those who have no one to speak up on their behalf.

We may wonder, does God really hear our prayers? God doesn't seem to hear the prayers of families caught up in the senseless violence of Syria, for example. God sometimes doesn't seem to hear our own prayers when we pray for a specific need. And yet, in the midst of God's silence, our faith challenges to trust ever more deeply in God's unconditional love for us. God is closer to us than we are to ourselves.

Paul, in his letter to Timothy, uses the imagery of sports to describe his own life and ministry, saying, "I have fought the good fight; I have finished the race; I have kept the faith; I will inherit the victor's crown as winners did in the games of ancient Greece and Rome." Despite many obstacles, Paul stays the course, preaching the Gospel in season and out of season (2 Tm 4:6–8, 16–18).

In the Gospel according to Luke, we have the odd couple. The Pharisee is full of himself: he fasted; he paid tithes; he kept the law. He thought that his laundry list of good works made him pleasing to God. But he was ego centered. Ego stands for "easing God out."

On the other hand, the tax collector recognized his dependency upon God's mercy. Tax collectors in the first century were generally judged by Jews as traitors or collaborators and detested by the Romans for pocketing money that could have been theirs. But the prayer of the tax collector was God centered, not ego centered. He knew that he was a flawed human being, less than perfect, less than forgiving. And so he prayed for God's mercy. He is the model of prayer for us, so says Jesus (Lk 18:9–14).

What fascinated me in today's readings is St. Paul's reflections about his life. Paul, we know, was well educated in Judaism and Greco-Roman philosophy. He had been a firebrand, a rabid persecutor of Christians. But Paul was suddenly blinded by a light from heaven. That awesome visionary experience of the risen Christ turned Paul's life upside down. He became God's chosen instrument to the non-Jews, one of the greatest evangelizers in Christianity.

Often controversial but always self-confident, Paul lived a purpose-driven life. This religious genius established Christian faith communities throughout the eastern Mediterranean, authored letters that shaped the history of Christian thought, and eventually was beheaded by Nero. But what was the secret to his purpose-driven life?

I like to think Paul, well versed in philosophy, had a keen insight into what makes human beings tick. Everyone yearns for happiness. That desire is universal. That's why we often do things that we think will make us happy, only to discover that they end up making us miserable. We confuse pleasure with happiness.

Etched into Paul's vision of human beings were the words of Jesus: "I have come so that they may have life, and have it more abundantly." For Paul, discipline is the path that leads to the fullness of life. Think about it. When we eat well, exercise often, and sleep regularly, we feel more fully alive physically. When we love, when we give priority to significant relationships, when we give of ourselves to help others, we feel more fully alive emotionally. When we study the achievements and marvels of the human spirit in various cultures, our world expands, and we feel more fully alive intellectually. And when we take a few moments each day to come before God in prayer, humbly and openly, we experience more fully the transcendent dimension of our lives, the spiritual.

But all of these endeavors require discipline. Discipline sets us free to attain our ultimate purpose: life with God. Freedom is not the ability to do whatever we want but is the strength of character to do what is good, true, noble, and right. Freedom is indeed a prerequisite for love.

Paul grasped this and preached that Christ came to reconcile us with the Father, and in doing so, Christ satisfies the craving for happiness that preoccupies our human hearts. Our yearning for happiness is ultimately a yearning for friendship and intimacy and relationship with our Creator. Augustine's words in the fifth century echo anew in every place, in every time, and in every heart: "Our hearts are restless until they rest in you, Lord." Christ, for Paul, is indeed "the way, the truth, and the life."

Who is this Jesus that captivated Paul and should captivate us?

The four Gospel writers give us a glimpse into four different portraits or faces of Jesus because they wrote to four different audiences and emphasized different ways in which to follow Jesus.

In Matthew, Jesus is the long-awaited Messiah, so Matthew reviews the family tree. Jesus emerges as the new Moses, the teacher, the rabbi who instructs the disciples in five discourses, and Matthew invites us to become teachers as well, especially by example, by the practice of virtue.

In Mark, Jesus is the suffering Messiah—very human, approachable.

Mark proposes that we, too, like the early Christians, may have to cope with suffering. And yes, we, like the early Christians, may wonder at times if God has forgotten us, especially if what's happening is the opposite of what we want.

In Luke, Jesus is compassionate and forgiving, and salvation is for everyone, not just Jews. Remember the parable of the prodigal son. Luke challenges us to be compassionate and forgiving in our relationships with one another.

In John, Jesus is noble, majestic, divine. "The Word was God." "Whoever has seen me has seen the Father." Jesus invites the first disciples to stay with him, and John invites us to stay with Jesus, especially in prayer.

Jesus is more than any one person can describe. What image of Jesus captivates us? What image inspires us to become the kind of person today that Jesus was in his day? Begin drawing your image of Jesus by meditating on the Gospels and let that image captivate you.

Thirty-First Sunday
in Ordinary Time

It's election season. I had a classmate at the Harvard Institutes, a Bostonian and a true believer in Beantown politics, who told me that when he died, he wanted to be buried in the South Boston cemetery so that he could continue to vote early and often.

Lyndon Johnson used to tell the story of two Texas ward healers who went to a cemetery just before an election to collect voters' names from the tombstones. They came to a tombstone so old and worn that the name was barely decipherable. "Let's forget that name," the first fellow shouted. The second fellow replied, "This man has as much a right to vote as the rest of these fellows here." That was politics in the good ole days. And some think it hasn't changed much today.

The book of Wisdom is a poetic and philosophical reflection about the meaning of life, the quest for true wisdom, God's grandeur and man's insignificance, mortality and immortality, and God's mercy and favor toward the oppressed Hebrews in ancient Egypt. These philosophical reflections were passed down from generation to generation and eventually compiled in the first century before Jesus into what we know today as the book of Wisdom.

Here the author speaks about the mighty God of this universe, creator of billions of galaxies with millions of stars in each galaxy, an awesome God completely beyond us and yet utterly within us, a God who is a lover of souls, a God who loves us unconditionally, forgives us unconditionally, and accepts us unconditionally. God, the author says, can be found everywhere: in the beauty of nature, in the changes of the seasons, and in people. The author's message here is simple: repent! Live an other-centered, God-centered life (Wis 11:22–12:2).

Paul in his letter prays that God will empower the Christian community in Thessalonika to continue doing good for others and to stop worrying about tomorrow. Seize the moment, Paul pleads (2 Thes 1:11–2:2).

A contemporary author, Pearl Yeadon McGinnis, paraphrased Paul well:

> I have no yesterdays ... time took them away;
> tomorrow may not be, but I have today.
>
> Make the most of today; practice random acts of kindness.
> Take time today to pray; it brings us closer to God.
> Take time to be friendly and hospitable; it's the source of much happiness; take time to work; it's the price of success.
> And take time to do acts of kindness; it's the key to heaven.
> Yes, we had yesterdays and may not have tomorrows; but we do have today. Make the best of it.

Good advice for all of us: make the best of today.

In the Gospel according to Luke, Jesus meets Zacchaeus, a tax collector and, in the eyes of first-century Jews, a scoundrel. His job was to tax his fellow Jews and ultimately turn these taxes over to their occupiers, the Romans, who denied many of their basic human rights. Yet Jesus here wants to stay at the house of Zacchaeus. His Jericho neighbors must have been shocked. *Doesn't Jesus know he works for the enemy, the Romans, and makes his money off fellow Jews?* But the call of Jesus became a transformative moment for Zacchaeus. From now on, he will be generous and honest (Lk 19:1–10).

We too can transform people into their best selves as Jesus transformed Zacchaeus. How? A good example, I think, is Dr. Karl Menninger, an internationally renowned twentieth-century psychiatrist. He was asked to visit a widow who had been depressed since her husband's death many years before. As they talked, Menninger noticed the beautiful violets she grew. So Menninger wrote an unusual prescription: the widow was to read her local newspaper every day and send a violet to someone who experienced a significant life event—the birth of a baby, marriage, graduation, a death in the family.

Within a month, the widow called Menninger and said her life had changed dramatically. She had become excited about life. She said every time she sent a violet, the receiver responded. The widow became known as the "violet lady" and began to live her life happily with new friends.

The point is simple. Jesus recognized the good in Zacchaeus that many in Jericho failed to see. The call of Jesus transformed his life. Christ calls us to transform others into their best selves in a similar fashion. How? By recognizing our gifts and abilities and using them to bring joy and peace and hope and forgiveness and consolation to others. That's what the violet lady did and what Jesus did, and that's what we can do—let the light of our faith in Jesus Christ shatter the darkness in other people, and help them manifest the glory of God within themselves.

Nelson Mandela said this clearly in his inaugural address as president of South Africa: "We were born to make manifest the glory of God within us. It's not just in some of us; it's in everyone. And as we let our own light shine, we unconsciously give other people permission to do the same: make manifest the glory of God within them."

Jesus challenged Zacchaeus and also challenges us to take stock of our lives, to examine our conscience about our priorities, what really matters in life.

But what is conscience? It is closely associated with our feelings. We sometimes feel guilty about things we do or don't do, and yet conscience is more than our feelings. It is a power of judgment. It's our way of judging whether our behavior and our attitudes are in sync with the way we ought to relate to God and to one another. Conscience, an informed conscience, is our moral compass, an almost instinctive judgment about the goodness or badness of our behavior and attitudes.

The Ten Commandments are one good guide for examining our conscience about how we relate to God, ourselves, other people, and things, so that we can realize our authentic selfhood. The commandments are really statements about freedom from attitudes and behaviors that undermine these relationships. They say very simply that our God is a God of love, and our response to God's unconditional love is, first and foremost, gratitude to God for who we are and what we have. We acknowledge our gratitude in worship. Moreover, this planet and the people on it reflect the image of God. And so all creation—human beings in particular—is worthy of reverence. God our Creator calls us creatures into relationship with himself, and that's why we give ourselves to God in weekly liturgies and in return receive God.

This same God challenges us to support virtues: for example, caring for aging parents; cherishing life from beginning to end; being faithful to our promises; speaking the truth; respecting the rights of others; not exploiting people; and being generous rather than greedy.

Someone observed, "You and I are writing our own gospel, a chapter each day, by the deeds we do, by the words we say." We might pray for the grace to be transformed into our best selves, like Zacchaeus, reflecting the presence and glory of God in our everyday attitudes and behavior.

Thirty-Second Sunday
in Ordinary Time

The e-mail saga in the presidential race is a cautionary tale about e-mails generally. For example, a couple decided to come to Florida for a long weekend to escape a cold and snowy winter in Minnesota. Both had jobs and couldn't coordinate their schedules so that they could fly together. The husband flew down first, checked into their favorite hotel, and found a computer. He decided to e-mail his wife. But he left out one letter in the address, and the e-mail accidentally went to a widow in Texas who just returned from her husband's funeral.

Now the Texas widow was checking her e-mails, expecting condolences. But she fainted upon reading the Minnesota husband's message. It read:

> To: My Loving Wife
> Subject: I've Arrived.
>
> I know you're surprised to hear from me, but they now have computers down here. I just arrived, and everything is ready for your arrival tomorrow. Looking forward to seeing you.
>
> P.S. It sure is hot down here.

So much for e-mails going to the wrong address.

The word of God takes us back in our imaginations to the second century before Jesus—the 100s. A foreign power—Syria—occupies Israel. And the king, Antiochus IV, is a tyrant—some would say a madman—determined to replace Jewish religious practices with Hellenic or Greek practices. The result is open rebellion. The author of the book of Maccabees describes the martyrdom of a mother and her seven sons. They stood up for their beliefs and died for them (2 Mc 7:1–2, 9–14).

The author may be asking us, do we stand up for what is right? Or do we simply go along to get along.

The author of the Letter to the Christian community at Thessalonika in Greece urges the community to stay the course, to persevere in their discipleship with Jesus. God will strengthen them, the author writes, so that they can fix their hearts on God and the things of God. That message is for us as well (2 Thes 2:16—3:5).

In the Gospel according to Luke, we have a dialogue between Jesus and the Sadducees about mortality and immortality. The Sadducees didn't believe in life after death. In this particular passage, they try to argue their case with an absurd example of seven brothers marrying the same sister-in-law and then each immediately dying. "Who's her husband in the next life?" the Sadducees ask. But Jesus turns the argument against them. He distinguishes between "this age" and "the next age." What if in the next life we are completely transformed into an utterly different reality? Moreover, even Moses alluded to life after death. Jesus here leaves the Sadducees dumbfounded (Lk 20:27–38).

The torture/martyrdom of the mother and her sons segues easily into the mystery of suffering from a Christian perspective. Our faith proclaims that hidden in every Good Friday is the glory of Easter.

We believe that the dead body-person of Jesus on Good Friday was transformed Easter dawn into a new awesome reality. Unlike a mortal body, the risen Christ could pass through walls; he could walk along a road and then "vanish." For the disciples, the resurrection of Jesus was real, even though they couldn't name his new mode of spiritual embodiment; it was a new phenomenon in their experience, of another world, as it were, within the life and power of God. And that new mode of spiritual embodiment one day will be ours.

In the meantime, we have our Good Fridays. Problems sometimes seem to overwhelm us. A family member loses a job, or is diagnosed with a severe illness, or sees a significant relationship begin to unravel. In such times, our faith challenges us to remember that the narrative of Jesus did not end in the tragedy of the cross but in the triumph of the resurrection.

In the midst of these problems or so-called bad luck, we may even wonder, *where is God?* This is an eternal question, highlighted in the biblical book of Job, in the autobiographical *Confessions* of the fifth-century Saint Augustine, in the literature of the Russian novelist Fyodor Dostoevsky, and in best sellers like Rabbi Harold Kushner's *When Bad Things Happen to Good People.*

Moreover, as we reflect upon the human situation today, violence in Syria and Iraq, the denial of basic human rights in some countries, poverty in Africa, we realize that the entire planet is wounded, so to speak, and cries out for a healer.

Yes, at times, suffering does result from immoral behavior, from the misuse of freedom. Adolph Hitler, Joseph Stalin, Mao Tse-Tung, and Pol Pot, for example, and many others created untold sufferings. At other times, suffering results from natural disasters like earthquakes in Italy and hurricanes in the Caribbean, from an unfinished, incomplete universe, a universe on the way, a universe in process toward an ultimate goal. But ultimately, suffering is a mystery. How do we respond to it?

First, we have to remember that God is always near us, closer to us than we are to ourselves. God forever seeks to bring us to the fullness of life. So, chisel in your consciousness the words of scripture, "Can a mother forget her child? And even if she does, I will never forget you."

Second, we should avoid negative judgments about ourselves if indeed we are experiencing bad luck, so to speak. To think, *I really deserve it,* is really a form of self-hatred. God loves us unconditionally.

Finally, we ought to remember that the mystery of inescapable suffering has healing and redemptive power. Why? Because Jesus, through the mystery of his horrible death and glorious resurrection, healed us, reconnected us to God in friendship. Yes, our everyday inescapable aches and pains, born with love, can be redemptive, can bring forth new depths of life in ourselves and in others. And why do I say this? Because the sufferings of Jesus brought forth a new and awesome transformed life for us.

So, as we conclude the week in which we commemorate all souls, how do we come to terms with our own dying? Most of us do not long with St. Paul "to be free from this earthly life so that we can be with the risen Christ." Many pass through Elizabeth Kubler Ross's stages of death and dying: denial, anger, bargaining, depression, and ultimately acceptance.

Stanford University helps people cope with the reality of death by encouraging them to begin drafting their last letter to loved ones. Stanford even developed a template that highlights the most important gifts we leave behind: love, faith in God, hope in life eternal, compassion, forgiveness, and gratitude. Check the template on the Internet.

In the Christian vision of things, we expect that the all-good God who continually amazes us will surprise us in the moment of our dying.

And so, as we reflect on the martyrdom of the mother and her sons in the book of Maccabees, let us recall that hidden in the dying of Jesus was the glory of his resurrection. And hidden within our own dying is the glory of eternal life. Death is not the end but a beginning of a new awesome life.

Thirty-Third Sunday
in Ordinary Time

A divided America has elected several new politicians. The serenity prayer may calm emotions: "God grant me the serenity to accept the things I cannot change, the courage to change the things I can, and the wisdom to know the difference … trusting that God will make all things right."

If you're into astronomy, look to the skies. Enjoy the grandeur of God!

Meanwhile, the next presidential election is in 2020. And if you're wondering where the country's going, I think of a story attributed, rightly or wrongly, to the late Supreme Court justice Oliver Wendell Holmes. He once boarded a train but couldn't find his ticket. The conductor reassured him. "Don't worry—you can send us the ticket after you reach your destination." Holmes responded, "The problem is not 'where's my ticket?' but 'where am I going?'" We may have similar feelings about our country. Certainly the Jews in the word of God today did.

The book of Malachi takes us back in our imaginations to the fifth century before Jesus. The author sees so much unethical behavior in ancient Israel that he proclaims a day of reckoning. On an unknown future day, God will act decisively, punish the wicked in a blazing fire and reward the good with the warm rays of the sun. Yes, God will hold us accountable, writes the author of Malachi (Mal 3:19–20).

Paul, in his letter to the Christians in Thessalonika, urges them to follow his example: he not only preaches the Gospel but also earns his own living. "Imitate me," Paul pleads. Don't be freeloaders, who goof off, grouse, and do nothing (2 Thes 3:7–12).

In the Gospel according to Luke, Jesus speaks about the destruction of Jerusalem's Temple. The temple was to Jerusalem what the Twin Towers were to New York City. Roman legions, putting down a rebellion, demolished the temple. The Jews were in shock, as New Yorkers were when terrorists demolished the Twin Towers in 2001. Jewish historian Josephus, who witnessed the Roman siege, tells of six thousand Jews perishing in the flames of the temple, and hundreds of thousands put to death, and almost one hundred thousand taken as prisoners (Lk 21:5–19).

For Luke, the end of Jerusalem was the prelude to the end of this world. The author uses apocalyptic imagery: wars and earthquakes, famines and plagues, persecutions and betrayals.

In the midst of all this, Jesus counsels us, "Persevere in your life of discipleship."

You may wonder why the word of God has all this gloom and doom. The answer is simple: we're at the end of the liturgical calendar.

The liturgical year relives the story of our salvation. We begin with Advent; we await a savior who came to us in Jesus of Nazareth in Bethlehem. We then walk the roads of Galilee and Judea with Jesus as he works signs and wonders, proclaiming that the kingdom of God was breaking into our midst.

We remember the Last Supper, the sacrificial death and glorious resurrection of Jesus, through whom we have a relationship with God. We relive the outpouring of the Spirit at Pentecost. And in the Sundays afterward, we witness the spread of the Gospel all over the Mediterranean—yes, even to Rome. And now, as we approach the end of the liturgical year, we wait in hope for the coming of the Lord Jesus again "in great power and glory," and next Sunday we will crown him king of the universe.

Yes, we celebrate in the liturgical year the story that began on the first page of Genesis: "In the beginning, God created the heavens and the earth," and that ends on the last page of Revelation: "Come, Lord Jesus." We await the second coming of the Lord Jesus. This universe as we know it will be transformed into a glorious kingdom in all its fullness, and that is why we proclaim, "Christ has died; Christ is risen; Christ will come again." How the universe will be transformed, whether in fire or ice, as Robert Frost describes in his remarkable poem, we don't know.

But the question is not how this planet will end. Rather the question is, are we ready when the risen Christ does come to us in the mystery of our own dying, either suddenly or gradually?

You may have read Harold Kushner's book *Living a Life That Matters*. In forty years as a rabbi, Kushner has cared for many people in their last moments. The people who had the most trouble with death, he wrote, were those who felt that they had never done anything worthwhile. If God would only give them another two or three years, maybe they would get it right. Death didn't frighten them; no, rather what worried them was the fear they would die without making a difference for the better in the lives of people.

The word of God asks, are we ready to face the risen Christ if he comes to us in the mystery of death today? If not today, when will we be ready? What behaviors do we have to change now? We know of course that there are some things we can do to delay our own appointment with death. We can exercise and eat the right foods. We can stop smoking and so on. But there's a basic truth in today's word of God. Ultimately, we all will have to keep an appointment with death. We will die at a particular time on a particular day in a particular year.

We don't know the day or hour of our own death. The news every day underscores this. People suddenly die in accidents or earthquakes or wars or hurricanes. We may be here one moment and gone the next. Life is precious and can be short—and so the urgency to try to live as best we can today as though it may be our last day.

"Be prepared" is not simply a scout motto; it's an everyday Christian motto.

The beatitudes can be a good guide in our everyday lives. Here's one paraphrase; think of your own paraphrases of the beatitudes:

"If you readily spend time listening and consoling others who look to you for support, for guidance, for compassion; if you manage to heal wounds and build bridges; if others see in you goodness, graciousness, joy, and serenity; if you can see the good in everyone and seek the good for everyone, blessed are you. You are nothing less than the face of God in our midst."

The word of God invites us to be prepared to face the risen Christ today. May that word inspire each one of us to value each day of our lives as a gift from God and to live each day as best we can, because today is the only day we can count on.

CHRIST THE KING SUNDAY

Thursday, we celebrate Thanksgiving, a remarkable story about people who never gave up in their quest for freedom of worship and speech, and freedom from fear and want. The day calls for gratitude to God that we are; and gratitude to our parents and grandparents, teachers, friends, and colleagues who made our lives possible; and gratitude to our nation for our freedoms and opportunities to realize our dreams.

I feel optimistic as we enter the Thanksgiving/Christmas season. I recall an anecdote about the parents who had twins, one always optimistic, the other always pessimistic. The parents went to a psychologist to better understand these two completely different personalities. The psychologist recommended this: for their birthday, buy the pessimist the best bicycle you can find; and for the optimist, go to the horse stable nearby and gather into a gift box the "stuff" you find on the stable floor.

When the twins opened their gifts, the pessimist began to whine about the bicycle, the color and lack of gadgets. Meanwhile, the optimist ripped open his box and gleefully giggled. "You can't fool me. There's gotta be a pony here somewhere." The moral of the story: be an optimist. Look for the good.

Today we celebrate the Feast of Christ the King, the one to whom we owe our ultimate allegiance, the Jesus who is the image of the invisible God, the crucified and risen Christ, through whom we have a relationship with God, the Christ who is the gateway to eternal life.

The late Supreme Court Justice Oliver Wendell Holmes Jr. was asked, "What has been the secret of your success?" Holmes responded, "At an early age, I discovered I was not God."

If only people throughout history discovered the same lesson, that they were not God. Rome's emperors thought they were living gods. Europe's medieval kings and queens boasted of their divine right. How do we rebut this mind-set?

Pope Pius XI in 1925, in the aftermath of World War I, which swept away four empires, was convinced that new dictators were emerging who thought they were God and would continue to deny people their basic human rights. So he wanted to point people to the one true God. That's how we have today's Feast of Christ the King.

The word "king" evokes all kinds of images. We may think of the pomp and circumstance of Elizabeth II when she opens up Parliament. Or of William Shakespeare's King Lear, old and foolish and mad, betrayed by two of his three daughters; if only they had family counseling! Or the overly passionate biblical King David and Bathsheba, or the not always so wise King Solomon and his many building projects, or the extravagant King Louis XIV of France and his chateau at Versailles, or some of the ceremonial kings and queens in our own twenty-first century. And yes, a few youngsters may even be thinking of Burger King.

Whatever image of king comes to mind may influence subconsciously our thoughts about this feast. But what, really, is this Feast of Christ the King all about?

In this feast, we reach the end of the liturgical year when, to quote the letter of Paul to the Christian community at Corinth, "every human being and all that is will be subjected to Jesus Christ, who will deliver the Kingdom of God over to his heavenly Father." Ours is a Christo-centric universe. God became incarnate in Jesus to share God's life and love and goodness with all creation.

The book of Samuel takes us back to the anointing of David as king of the northern tribes of Israel at the sacred shrine of Hebron, where Abraham centuries before had built an altar to God. The people acknowledge their kinship with the king. He will be their watchful shepherd as well as their wise leader. As we reflect upon David's anointing, we also might reflect upon our own anointing at baptism, in which we were consecrated and set apart to live a life worthy of our calling as sons and daughters of God our Father (2 Sm 5:1–3).

The letter of Paul to the Christian community at Colossae in Turkey highlights probably an early Christian hymn of thanksgiving to God and exaltation of Jesus. The first stanza describes Christ before his birth. He is the image of the invisible God, the model or blueprint after which all things were fashioned. The second stanza describes Christ after his earthly life. He is the beginning, the firstborn of the dead, the head of the church through whose dying/rising we're in relationship with God. Christ, the God-man, completely divine and completely human, moves from heaven to earth and back to heaven. Against some false ideas in the first century of our Christian era, the author proclaims that Christ alone is the ruler of the universe (Col 1:12–20).

In the Gospel according to Luke, we reexperience the theme of "rise and downfall" in two criminals. We remember how Simeon prophesized in Luke's infancy narrative that the child in his arms was destined to be the downfall and rise of many. One can also interpret this theme in the parable of the prodigal son (one repentant, the other unforgiving) and the two men at prayer in the Jerusalem Temple (one haughty, the other repentant). Lo and behold, again we meet one man who asks for forgiveness, another who doesn't. One rises ("this day you will be with me in Paradise"), and the other apparently meets his downfall (Lk 23:35–43).

And above the head of the crucified Jesus is the mocking inscription: "This is the King of the Jews."

We as a community of faith profess our ultimate allegiance to Jesus Christ. We say that we prize this relationship with Jesus. And so we might ask ourselves, how do we spend our time, our energy, our resources? Do we spend them with Jesus in prayer and in service to one another? Or are we simply absorbed in ourselves and the things of this earth?

I like the quote, "I shall pass through the world but once: any good therefore that I can do or any kindness that I can show to any human being, let me do it now, let me not defer or neglect it, for I shall not pass this way again."

Jesus calls us to an ongoing conversion, a change of heart, a turning away from a self-centered life and a turning toward an other or God-centered life.

The Russian novelist Feodor Dostoevsky wrote in *The Brothers Karamazov* that men and women of faith want to believe in someone or something that is ultimately true.

We proclaim that Jesus is our truth. But do we really believe it? What is our first priority? What makes us tick? God and the things of God? Or merely the things of this earth?

This feast asks us, how can we rededicate ourselves ever more deeply to Jesus, our way, our truth, and our life? Yes, how can be better nurture that relationship with God so that in the mystery of our own dying, we can rise with the risen Christ into a new, transformed heavenly life?

Bibliography

Alighieri, Dante. *The Divine Comedy*. 1320

Boren, Marcelle. *Disorder in the American Courts*, Iwahu Publishing, 2016.

Edelman, Marian Wright. *Lanterns: A Memoir of Mentors*. Beacon Press, 1999.

Francis of Assisi—The Saint: Early Documents. Vol. 1. New City Press, 1999.

Heller, David. *Dear God: Children's Letters to God*. Perigee Trade, 1994.

Heschel, Abraham Joshua. *I Asked for Wonder: A Spiritual Anthology*. The Crossroad Publishing Company, 1983.

Kelley, Jack. USA Today reporter, from "The Stories Behind the Headlines," given at Evangelical Press Association convention, May 2000.

Kozol, Jonathan. *Amazing Grace: The Lives of Children* and *Conscience of a Nation*. Crown Publishing, 1995.

Kozol, Jonathan. *Ordinary Resurrections: Children in the Years of Hope*. Crown Publishing, 2000.

Kushner, Harold S. *Living a Life That Matters*. Anchor, 2002.

Levy, Naomi. *Hope Will Find You.* Harmony Books, 2010.

Morrow, Lance. *The Chief: A Memoir of Fathers and Sons.* Macmillan Pub Co, 1986.

O'Connor, Flannery. *Everything that Rises Must Converge* – "Revelation." Farrar Straus Giroux, 1965.

Powell, John, S.J. *Through Seasons of the Heart.* Thomas More Pub., 1987.

Schweitzer, Albert. *The Philosophy of Civilization.* Prometheus Books, 1987 (first published 1923).

Ten Boom, Corrie. *The Hiding Place.* Bantam Books, 1974.

Mother Teresa of Calcutta quotes from the archives of the Missionaries of Charity.

Warren, Rick. *The Purpose Driven Life.* Zondervan, 2002.

Welch, Myra Brooks. "The Touch of the Master's Hand." In *The Gospel Messenger.* Brethren Press, 1921.

Weisenthal, Simon. *The Sunflower: On the Possibilities and Limits of Forgiveness.* Schocken, 1998.

"Christ Has No Hands But Our Hands," words by Annie J. Flint, Music by Tom Eggleston, 1986

A Civil Action. DVD. 1999.

A Raisin in the Sun, DVD, 2000.

Brooklyn, DVD, 2015.

42: The Jackie Robinson Story, DVD, 2013.

Printed in the United States
By Bookmasters